BLEEDING HEARTS

A True Story of Alzheimer's, Family, and the Other Woman

SECOND EDITION

Tami A Reeves

ISBN: 1973825309
ISBN 13: 9781973825302

AUTHOR'S NOTE

I began this book as a journal. I, being the "other woman", had difficult days of my own so I took to journaling my feelings as an outlet. It was before I put pen to paper, so to speak, that I realized that my journey could be beneficial to others. Beneficial in a way to help society become more aware of other's needs and less judgmental towards those moving in their grief. For society to see that a support person, such as I was, is more than what they might judge them to be. That they are, in fact, just that, support for someone, during the worst of times.

Because of the situation I was in, my eyes were opened wider than they had ever been before. Being a pediatric and trauma nurse, I have seen my share of suffering and pain. Not only by my patients, but by their family members. I have always been drawn to them, reaching out to provide support while they were witnessing some heart breaking life events. It's the family members who are often forgotten in these times. But not always, which is part of the problem.

Often times they are supported as long as they follow society's rules. I have lived my life, for the most part, as society has dictated.

But in my growth, as a human being, I see that often times, society is gravely wrong. Marriage vows are sacred, I believe that. But I also believe that in difficult times a person needs to do whatever it takes to get them through the tough time, without disrespecting the loved one who is suffering. And that person, should be allowed to do so without facing persecution from others.

The fact that Eric decided to find a companion, at the insistence of his daughter (she is the one who set up his online dating profile), was seen, by many, as not respecting his wife and/or vows of his marriage. Eric wasn't looking for a floosy or one night stand. He was looking for a partner, not to replace his beautiful wife, but to share the rest of his life with and, hopefully, help him weather the storm he was caught in. Regardless of what he felt his needs were, he should be allowed to move in his journey the way he needed to, without persecution.

And of course, that judgement extended to me. While I spent countless days at the nursing home with Gaye (by myself), tried to be there for her children and grandchildren, and tried keeping Gaye's memory alive; what I was doing was seen as shameful and not supportive.

In writing and publishing this book I hoped to begin a movement in society that recognizes everyone's needs are different. Because seeing, first hand, the discrepancies in support and judgements against people moving in their own grief, warranted the conversation to start. Not just the conversation between two partners, but in society as a whole. To begin to accept a person's needs during their journey with their suffering loved one. To see what that support person actually is to them and their family, instead of holding on to rigid ideas that, while still honorable, can't and don't dictate how everyone should handle a crisis such as losing a loved one to Alzheimer's.

I have had some success with the acceptance of what I propose with this book. I know of one gentleman who, after his wife passed from Alzheimer's, used my book in many of his support groups and even quoted from it when he spoke at such groups. This, I know, is just a tip of the iceberg. But it warms my heart knowing that there are some people, caught in this struggle, being given the support they need to move on the way they see fit.

I realize that not everyone needs or even wants to "move on" in a situation such as ours. But if they are so moved, they should be allowed to do it without judgement or ridicule from society. The difficulties I faced were just that, judgement. Judgment by those who had no idea of what Eric, his family or I were living. My hope is we all learn to do what is right for us in that time of need, without judgement but with full support and love because...

"Everyone's journey is their own..."

CONTENTS

Preface	ix
Prologue	xi
Chapter 1 ~ A Sailor and His Love	1
Chapter 2 ~ Childhood Sweethearts	14
Chapter 3 ~ The Nightmare Begins	26
Chapter 4 ~ The Diagnosis	40
Chapter 5 ~ Moving On	54
Chapter 6 ~ Mending a Broken Heart	63
Chapter 7 ~ Love Moving Quickly	72
Chapter 8 ~ Meeting Gaye and the Family	81
Chapter 9 ~ Christmas!	87
Chapter 10 ~ Unlocking the Pain	95
Chapter 11 ~ Motorcycles, Europe and a New House	100
Chapter 12 ~ The "Big" Gift	110
Chapter 13 ~ Difficult Decisions	115
Chapter 14 ~ Continued Pain	122
Chapter 15 ~ The Beginning of the End	137
Chapter 16 ~ Love and Her Sailor	150
Chapter 17 ~ Progressing	156
Chapter 18 ~ The Memorial	165
Chapter 19 ~ One Last Difficult Time	174
Chapter 20 ~ A Connection from Beyond	183
Chapter 21 ~ Bleeding Hearts in Bloom	194

PREFACE

When Alzheimer's strikes, it changes lives forever. In their concern for the patient, health care workers and society in general often overlook the other victims of the disease—the family. Alzheimer's takes its toll on spouses, children, and other family members who must stand by—helpless and heartbroken—as they watch their loved one suffer. *Bleeding Hearts* is the true story of one such family and how they battled with, and ultimately triumphed over, this devastating disease.

PROLOGUE

As Gaye dug up the last plant, her grandmother appeared at her side. Gaye placed the freshly uprooted plant into the container already filled with several of the healthy-looking plants. "Is that all you want?" her grandmother asked her. "There's plenty more if you need them. I know how much you've always loved them."

"No, Grandma, this is plenty. I can't wait to plant them at home, and when they all take root, my whole yard will be filled with bleeding hearts! And you're right—they are one of my favorite flowers!"

For as long as Gaye could remember, bleeding hearts had filled her grandmother's and her mother's yards in Idaho Falls. And now she, too, wanted them in the yard of her new home in Colorado. She'd grown up admiring how they displayed their pink colors, dangling on a branch and catching the breeze. Upon arriving home, she promptly set to planting the twenty-plus plants that she'd brought with her. She and her husband, Eric, quickly found a home for them all. "They'll be beautiful soon," Gaye told him.

Year after year, the plants bloomed and grew larger. They were happy in their new home and Gaye couldn't have been more thrilled. One beautiful summer day, she was outside admiring the flowers she loved so much, when she heard the phone ring. It was her mother.

"Gaye, the doctor thinks it's time to move Grandma into a nursing home," she said through her tears.

"Has it really gotten that bad?" Gaye asked.

"It's worse than you can imagine," her mother said. "When we moved her in here with me three years ago, I could take care of her. But now she thinks I'm out to get her and doesn't remember who I am. Gaye, it's just breaking my heart that my own mother doesn't even know me anymore. Alzheimer's is a horrible disease. It's robbing me of my mother before she's even gone!" Gaye's mother broke down in tears.

Gaye felt her own tears rolling down her cheek and the gnawing pain in her heart that had begun when they had gotten the diagnosis four years ago. Gaye was extremely close to her grandmother and grandfather (who had passed some years before), and the day that she had first heard about the diagnosis was a day she wanted to forget. "Oh Mom, what can I do?" she asked through her own tears.

"Your sister and I are looking for a place now. We'll make sure to find one that will take good care of her, I promise," her mother told her.

As Gaye hung up the phone, Eric stood in front of her. "What is it?" he asked.

"Grandma's going into a nursing home!" she blurted out as she buried her head into his chest sobbing. He held her tight, trying to ease away her pain and tears. "Eric, what if I get Alzheimer's? Now that we know Grandma has it, I could end up with it. Please tell me I won't get it," she pleaded, her head still buried deep into him.

"Of course you won't, Gaye; just because she has it doesn't mean you'll get it," he tried to reassure her.

"I can't stand the thought of my grandmother in a nursing home," she told him. "I can't bear her deteriorating and not knowing me or anyone. This is so horrible, Eric; Alzheimer's is so unfair!"

Over the next four years, Gaye made several trips to visit her grandmother. She was horrified to witness the once-vibrant woman, full of life and love, now trapped in the shell of her outer body. Difficult though it was for Gaye to see her grandmother's condition, her love for the older woman overpowered her sorrow. Not only could her grandmother not speak, but she was also bedridden, and with each successive visit, Gaye saw that she had lost more weight. Every time Gaye left the care facility, she said a prayer that her grandmother would be free of her body soon and that her suffering, as well as Gaye's own, would end.

The day finally came when Gaye received the phone call she'd been waiting for. Her dear sweet grandmother was finally free. Released from the body in which she had become a prisoner, without even the slightest recollection to warm her heart, she could now reclaim the memories she'd had before the relentless disease took over her mind. And now her family was free as well—free from the pain of watching their loved one suffer as the disease brutally took over her mind and body—and free at last from the anguish of their own bleeding hearts.

CHAPTER 1

A SAILOR AND HIS LOVE

"Gaye, this is the third time this week you've forgotten your password," said Anne, the IP person at the firm where Gaye worked.

"I know, I guess it's just all the excitement of planning for Europe and all," Gaye replied. "I just seem so forgetful lately!"

"Are you and Eric really moving there?" Anne asked.

"Yes, we leave in December! We're so excited. We've wanted to do this for a long time. I'm quitting work in a few weeks so I can start to get things ready."

"Aren't you going to miss the kids and grandkids?"

"Yes, but we'll have them all come out! What a joy it will be to show them Europe!"

The weeks flew by. As Gaye prepared to pack her personal items from her desk, she glanced at the calendar that was in front of her. Noting the date, September 1, 2000, she realized how long she had been working at the stationery company. "I started here in 1985," she recalled. "Wow, fifteen years—the time has flown by!"

Gaye continued to clear out the last of her desk drawers and packed her things in a cardboard box. She stopped to study an old picture of herself and Eric; she couldn't help shaking her head at how far they had come over the years together. As she stared at their younger faces, elusive memories flitted through her mind and she tried to capture them, if only for just a moment. She and Eric had met a long time ago, she knew that much, but concentrate though she might, she couldn't recall the exact date or circumstances of when the photo was taken. After some minutes, she rubbed her forehead as if to ease the tension and, for the time being, abandoned the effort of remembering. With care, she placed the photograph in the box and, her excitement rising, she thought, "We'll have many more pictures to add to this one when we tour Europe."

It was fall 1973, and Eric, a naval seaman, was with his buddies in a local bar in Bremerton, Washington. He had been to this town before during his tour and always enjoyed it. He and his buddies took seats in the dark, dusty bar that smelled of beer, whisky and stale cigarette smoke. Eric, stroking his long beard, looked around the bar and spotted a table with three attractive young women sitting around playing cards. Eric was most taken by a pretty blonde with big blue eyes and, when she caught his gaze, she smiled.

"Hey, go over there, man!" Eric's buddy John egged him on. "She's definitely into you, go talk to her!"

"Nah, she's just being nice" Eric said.

"That was more than a 'being nice' smile. I think she digs you. Go talk to her. What would it hurt?"

Eric entertained the thought for a moment as he continued to look at her.

"That guy has the prettiest eyes I've ever seen," Gaye said to her friend Stacie.

"Well, he won't quit looking over here; apparently he thinks something like that about you. Why don't you go ask him to play cards with us? His friend is kind of cute too; ask them both," Stacie said.

"Which one?" Gaye asked.

"The one with the blonde beard next to him. Go ask them and I'll order another pitcher of beer."

Gaye stood up from the table and straightened out her skirt. She was a pretty girl, thin with long blonde hair and big blue eyes. Her smile lit up her face when she was happy, but it had been a while since she had been happy. Her divorce had been quick and uncomplicated. She and her daughter, Melanie, had settled in with her parents, Ila and Mac (her stepfather), after she'd left her abusive husband on the East Coast. Life was going to be better now that she was away from him. She was looking forward to finding the happiness to light up her smile again.

She approached Eric's table and introduced herself. Eric extended his hand. "Nice to meet you. These are my friends John, David and Sam."

Gaye shook hands with everyone and said, "My girlfriends and I were playing cards and thought maybe you guys would like to join us."

Eric wasted no time accepting the invitation. "John?" he said, cocking his head in the direction of Gaye's table.

"Sure," John said. "Kind of boring sitting at a table with all guys when there's a table with so many pretty girls!"

As they crossed the bar, Eric couldn't take his eyes off her. She was the prettiest thing he had ever seen. Eric wasn't much of a card player, but he was anxious to get to know this girl with the pretty blue eyes. As they sat down and went through the motions of dealing cards, the game was soon forgotten when conversation took over.

"So you're in the navy. How do you like it?" Gaye asked.

"Well, not by choice. I was drafted. I was going to the School of Mines in Colorado and, well, partied too much and was asked to leave. I then enrolled in another college, but Uncle Sam called for me," Eric explained.

"In Colorado? Is that where you're from?" she asked.

"Well, not really, I'm from all over. My dad was in the air force. I graduated high school in Colorado Springs but did a lot of my growing up in Europe".

"Gaye's voice rose with excitement. "Europe! "I've always wanted to go there. Did you love it?"

"I guess. I was a kid mostly and really didn't appreciate it. I want to go back someday, maybe even live there. I don't know what the future will bring, but I can't do anything until I get out of the navy. Uncle Sam has me for the next twenty-one months; that's when my three-year tour will be over."

Just then, the jukebox started to play "Smoke on the Water" loud enough to make conversation difficult. Eric nodded to John and motioned that they were going outside. John smiled and went back to talking with Stacie.

"So have you lived here long?" Eric asked as they walked outside into the cool damp night.

In Bremerton, a town on the water, the air was often damp, especially this time of year when the weather was turning cooler. Leaves had started falling and there was a chill to the air.

"No, I recently moved here from the East Coast," Gaye explained. To her surprise she felt comfortable sharing the details of her former marriage with Eric. Somehow, he didn't feel like a stranger that she'd only known an hour or so.

"How old is your daughter?" Eric asked.

"Just a little over a year old. She's adorable—she's my world and the reason I left my ex. I wanted her to have a better life than what we were living. She's the only good thing that came from that relationship," Gaye said.

"I'm glad," Eric said, "not that you had to endure so much, but that you got out. If you hadn't, I wouldn't be sitting here with you now."

They both smiled and sat down on a bench near the water. In the distance there was a fog rolling in, and a light breeze was blowing. Gaye shivered and moved closer to Eric.

"I'd offer you my jacket, but I didn't bring one. Here, maybe this will help keep you warm," he said as he slid his arm around her shoulder. She leaned against him, feeling his warm body melting her chills away.

Gaye wanted to have an early night, and Eric suggested that he walk her home. But she had already arranged to ride with her friends. "Maybe I could see you tomorrow," she said, surprised at her own boldness. She also offered to pick him up at his ship.

"I'm not staying on the ship. My buddies and I have a small apartment on Second Street. It's right above the tavern there in Port Orchard," he said.

They agreed that Gaye would pick him up at the apartment around five the next afternoon. He walked her to her friend's car and hugged her goodnight. As the two waved good-bye, she felt a stirring of the old happiness she'd known before her abusive marriage. She smiled as she thought about her next meeting with Eric.

Over the next few days, Gaye and Eric were inseparable. They discovered that they had much in common and talked about everything. Gaye was at ease with this tall, handsome sailor, not typical for her because she was often shy, but Eric made her feel as though she were confiding in an old friend. They spent hours just taking walks and talking. When they were walking close together, with his arm around her, she felt warm and safe, as if she belonged at his side. The cool, damp autumn air didn't seem to touch her as long as Eric was next to her—only the smell of damp brown leaves reminded her it was fall.

Each night, as he slipped back into bed at the apartment, Eric would wonder about this beautiful girl. Everything felt so right with her, but how could that be? Though they had just met, he felt like he had known her for a long time. She had a daughter, which wasn't a complication but something to think about. As he drifted off to sleep, it was with thoughts of Gaye and the smell of her perfume on his mind. He wondered what Gaye was thinking at that exact moment.

She had stroked his beard tonight; did it mean that she liked it or that she didn't? It was quite long these days, as he had let it grow out for a while. "Maybe it's time for me to get rid of it," he thought. "I'll ask Gaye what she thinks of it tomorrow," he muttered to himself as he succumbed to sleep.

There was one big shadow over the budding romance. Eric was shipping out soon.

"Before you go, I'd like you to meet my mom, stepdad and Melanie," Gaye said as they strolled along the beach of the harbor. It was the afternoon before Eric's departure.

"I'd love to meet your parents. Should I shave my beard before I meet them?" he asked.

She turned to face him, her hand holding one of his and stroking his beard with her other hand, admiring how soft it felt. "I'll never talk to you again if you do," she said. "I told you a couple of days ago that I love your beard, and they'll like you fine, beard and all. I'll make dinner and you can come over at six tonight. OK?" she asked.

He wrapped his arms around her in a warm embrace. "I can't wait to meet them, especially Melanie," he told her. "But I need to get back to the ship to get some things in order before we ship out. Then I'll change and head over for dinner at your mom's place."

"I hate that you're going tomorrow; it feels like you just got here," she said as tears welled up in her eyes.

"I know, but let's not think about it yet. Let's just enjoy tonight and take tomorrow as it comes," he told her, trying to ease his own feelings as well as hers.

"I've got to be the luckiest man in the world. I have a beautiful girl that I'm crazy about who is cooking me dinner tonight," Eric thought to himself as he got ready for dinner. His anticipation of being with Gaye that evening calmed any anxiety about meeting her parents.

As he approached the front steps of Gaye's mom's house, it finally dawned on him that he was going to meet her parents, and the nerves set in. As he rang the bell, he fidgeted with his hair and beard. The door opened, and there she was, the beautiful creature with a happy smile, a smile that seemed different than it had been the first time they met.

As she drew him in, she kissed his cheek. The smell of fried chicken filled the air as he let Gaye lead him into the kitchen. She introduced him to her mother, Ila, a tall woman with the same blue eyes as Gaye's.

The three of them were making conversation when Gaye's stepfather, Mac, walked in carrying a blonde-haired toddler. Gaye took the toddler from her stepfather and turned to Eric. "This is Melanie," she said, hugging her. The happy toddler had the same blue eyes as her mother and grandmother, he noticed. She squealed as her mother hugged her tight. "What a happy little girl," Eric thought to himself.

⟡

After dinner and conversation, Gaye and Eric excused themselves to go for a drive. They drove to a spot with a beautiful view of the harbor. "I still can't believe you're leaving tomorrow. When will you be back again?" Gaye asked while parking the car.

"I'll be at sea for nine months. I'll write, Gaye, I promise I will. Tell me you'll write me too," Eric pleaded, feeling desperate at the thought of not being near her.

"Of course I will; I'll miss you, though," she said, fighting back tears.

"I'll miss you too," he said as he pulled her to him "But the way it looks now, when we return, the ship will be docked in Port Orchard for five months."

Gaye's face lit up, and she wrapped her arms around his neck in a tight squeeze. "I'll be counting the days until then," she said as she looked into his eyes and kissed him.

Eric gently pulled her back so her eyes met his. "While I'm gone I'll write and will cherish every letter you send me. But it's selfish of me to expect you to wait here for me. I want you to go on and live your life as normal. If that means you meet someone else, then so be it. But when I come back in the spring—if you're still available and we both have the same feelings—we'll pick up from here. Agreed?" he asked.

"That sounds fair, Eric, but I'll be anxiously looking for your return," she said, and they kissed again.

⟡

For Eric, out at sea, and for Gaye, back in Port Orchard, the months dragged on. They exchanged a few letters. But they each continued to live their lives apart.

Finally, the waiting was over. Eric sent a letter to Gaye telling her when he'd be in port and that he'd like to see her as soon as possible. "I'll be waiting at the end of the pier for you," she told him in her last letter. The day the ship arrived, Eric was lost in thoughts of Gaye. As he walked down the pier, he worried that she might have forgotten. But true to her word, there she was—the beautiful, golden-haired beauty he remembered. He hurried down the pier to her waiting arms.

Pulling away from the loving embrace, Gaye said, "Eric, I want to show you my new house. I'm renting a small place for Mel and me. She's with my mom tonight. I'll fix you dinner and fill you in on what's happened since you've been gone. I'm so glad you're here!"

Eric worked on board ship during the day, but every night and weekend, he spent with Gaye and Mel in the little rented house. Their love grew; they lived as a family and experienced a love more powerful than either of them would ever have imagined they could feel.

The weeks turned into months, and as the end of the fifth month approached, Eric reminded Gaye that he would soon have to leave.

"I know, Eric, but this time seven months won't be so long and then you'll be here to stay. The nine months were hard, in part because I had only a few days with you then. But now, after spending so much time together, I have so much to remember that will keep you close to me." Despite her optimism and attempts to be brave, she could not hold back her tears.

"We still have next weekend; we'll make every moment that we're together count and not let them go," he said as he tried to soothe her obvious pain.

By the next weekend, Eric realized that he couldn't expect Gaye to wait again for him and urged her to date if she were interested in someone while he was away. Even though they had such strong feelings for each other, he felt that it was unfair to expect her to wait for him.

"Eric, that's ridiculous! Of course I'll wait for you," she said sternly.

"I know that your heart says that now, but Gaye, honestly, if you meet someone, don't think twice about me. I just want you to be happy. I want the best for you and Melanie. Promise me," he said with an ache in his heart.

"Whatever you say, Eric, but I know I'll wait," she assured him.

This time, Eric wrote almost every day. He wrote of his feelings for Gaye and Melanie and about what he hoped their lives would be like when he got back. He phoned a couple of times when he was able. The deep ache in his heart for Gaye let him know how much he really loved her.

The seven months were nearing an end, and Eric couldn't wait to get back to Gaye. But lately, there were fewer and fewer letters from her. Two weeks from the end of his tour, Eric called Ila's house, looking for Gaye.

He was heartbroken to find out that Gaye had been seeing another man. All the months of being on ship, dreaming of their future life together, was for nothing. Eric, feeling desperate, decided to make one last plea for Gaye. The next two weeks felt longer than the entire seven months at sea. Eric worried every day about losing Gaye; his love for her was so deep that he at least had to tell her one last time how he felt.

Once in Bremerton, Eric learned that Gaye was camping with the man she'd been seeing. He made up his mind that he would park outside her house and wait for them to return. Not knowing what time they would arrive, Eric was prepared to stay all day if he needed to. He wasn't leaving until he, at the very least, talked to her. He wanted to know from her, firsthand, that she no longer had feelings for him.

Not long after he'd arrived, a Jeep pickup pulled up with a man driving and Gaye in the passenger seat. Eric's heart felt heavy. Gaye came out of the truck, and Eric heard the man say something to her but couldn't make out the words. She motioned for him to leave and he drove off. Gaye approached Eric and soon they were face-to-face.

"So, Gaye, do you want to be with him—or with me? You need to make a choice," Eric said, almost afraid to hear what she would say.

"You, Eric. I want—no—I need to be with you," she said through her tears.

He swept her into his arms. "I've been so worried. I didn't know what to think over the last two weeks," he said as he held her in a tight embrace.

"Listen, Gaye, I'm leaving for Colorado in a few days to see my parents and figure out what I'm going to do. I want you and Melanie to come with me," he said.

"I can't Eric, I can't. I'm in the middle of the semester." Gaye had enrolled in some classes to help pass the time. "I can't just pick up and leave. I have obligations and commitments here right now," she said, crying.

It was then that Eric picked her up and carried her to the car. "Sure you can, see how easy it is?" he said. They both burst into laughter and held each other.

"OK, I'll go to Colorado as planned. Then we'll come up with a plan, Gaye. We'll get this all figured out. I promise."

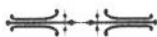

Once in Colorado, Eric was miserable, despite being glad to see his family. At breakfast one morning, he decided to confide in his mother about his plans.

"I thought I should come here to figure things out, and I think I have," he told her. "I'm going to buy a car and go back to Port Orchard. I can get a job in the shipyard, I'm sure. I need to be with her, Mom—I love her."

Once back in Port Orchard, Eric moved into the small duplex with Gaye and Melanie. Life seemed so right. Not long afterward, he got a job as a rigger in the shipyard and soon applied to the electronics apprentice program. Things were going the way he had hoped. They were building a life together and, with the training he was getting, he could offer his new family a better future. They soon moved into a trailer on a lake. The future was unfolding as it should, except for one thing.

"Gaye," Eric said while they were sitting on the couch watching TV one evening, "I think it's time we got married. What do you think?" he asked.

"I've been waiting for you to say something!" Gaye said. "I'd love to have a fall wedding, maybe in my grandmother's backyard. It wouldn't cost much and my grandmother said she would make the cake. You could have your brother be best man; my sister can be my maid of honor. It'll be a lovely wedding!"

Eric smiled at her excitement. "Well! You've been thinking about this for a while. Sounds like the plans are made. All I have to do is show up!" he kidded her.

They were married on September 25, 1976, in Gaye's grandmother's backyard. Both families gathered to celebrate the occasion. It was a beautiful fall day. Eric anxiously awaited Gaye's descent toward him down the makeshift aisle. When he saw her, she looked like an angel and took his breath away. "This is perfect," he thought to himself as Gaye approached. I have the love of my life and a little girl; we will have a wonderful life, building memories together. I must be the luckiest man in the world."

Over the next year, their family expanded. They adopted a dog and found out Gaye was expecting a baby. "The baby is due in February," Gaye told Eric excitedly. "I can't believe our good fortune!"

"Gaye, with another Reeves on the way, maybe it's time we thought about making Melanie a Reeves. Officially, I mean," Eric said as he joined in the excitement.

The adoption papers were final a few days after Gaye and Eric welcomed their precious baby boy, Eric Jr.—or Rix, as the family calls him—into the world. They soon bought a new home that would be big enough for their growing family. It was located on a cul-de-sac with great neighbors that soon became friends. They all shared BBQs and card nights, and their children played together. The years passed and the children grew, as did Eric and Gaye's love.

Eric finished his apprenticeship, but the Washington winters were beginning to take a toll on him and his well-being. He longed to live in Colorado again. Since Gaye's mom and Mac had moved back to Idaho, Eric had begun thinking about relocating the family to Colorado. Late one summer, they decided to sell the house and move to Colorado. It was almost September and school was starting soon; they needed to settle into a home and get Melanie enrolled.

They finally found a place and Melanie began fifth grade. Eric got a job working at Cheyenne Mountain as a civilian. He also began night school to pursue his electronics engineering degree. The family moved once again, into a bigger home, and Eric graduated. Life was going well for this family. The children were thriving and Eric had many promotions; he finally left "the mountain," as they called it, to pursue his career on a military base located in Colorado Springs.

Melanie married young, at age nineteen, and had a baby boy, Nathan. The marriage, like most young marriages, soon ended and Mel, as the family refers to her, moved to Idaho to live with her grandmother. She soon met Jamie and married him and gave birth to twin boys. During this time, Rix was attending the Colorado School of Mines, where he met Emily, the girl that would become his bride. Once Rix graduated, Eric and Gaye announced to the family that they were moving to Europe.

CHAPTER 2
CHILDHOOD SWEETHEARTS

At the time that Gaye and Eric were packing for Europe, I was living in Colorado Springs with my then husband, Tim. I had not met Gaye or Eric at this time, but we later found out that we had common acquaintances. I had worked at the stationery factory when Gaye was also employed there, and Eric had once driven home a colleague who lived two houses away from us. In addition, I later got a job at a hospital near Eric's workplace.

It was the year 2000 and my life centered on my children, my work in the family business and trying to hold together my failing marriage. My husband, Tim, and I had many apparent strengths in our relationship but, deep down, something was missing. Eventually we would both have to face this truth.

⁂

Tim and I met as children. We are both CODAS (Children of Deaf Adults). My mom went to the deaf school in Colorado Springs with Tim's parents. He and I met on an Easter weekend; I was six and he was eight. We drove from our home in Texas to their home in Colorado to spend Easter with my mom's former schoolmates and longtime friends.

We arrived early Friday morning before Easter and met Patty and Melvin, my mother's friends. After a little while, a sleepy-eyed little girl with long brown hair came into the living room, rubbing her eyes. She took a seat on her father's lap and studied my siblings and me as we sat in her family's living room. A few minutes after she arrived, Tim, also sleepy eyed, but blond haired and blue eyed, came in and sat next to his mom on a chair. We all looked at each other. There was an ease about meeting fellow CODAs, a familiarity that made us all feel like we knew each other, even though we were meeting for the first time. Nothing seemed uncomfortable; we were with another "deaf" family. The children weren't deaf, but the parents were. It was very "same" for us, as the deaf would call it. It is the same with all CODAs when we meet—we are from "deaf," so it is all familiar and everyone is family. The friendships are already in place, because our parents are deaf.

"You must be Tim," one of my siblings said. He nodded his head and smiled.

"And you're Tammy!" I said to the little girl, excited to meet someone with the same name. "So are you," said Tammy. We all laughed. I then introduced my younger sister, Naomi, and then introduced my brother, Sammy. After a few moments, Tammy said, "Want to see my room?"

She and I headed to her room with my little sister in tow. We had a very nice weekend, complete with Easter candy, Easter dinner and an egg hunt. Looking back, I realize that something felt very familiar with the family, something other than the "deafness".

Back at home, it was life as usual. When I was growing up in the 1960s, there were no laws for interpreters for the deaf. We had no fax machines, Internet or even TTDs (Teletypewriting Devices). Because of my signing ability, my parents decided early on that they would depend on me to be their link to the hearing world, which was the norm at the time. It was usually the oldest of the hearing children who would take on this role, but because of my skill, my parents gave the responsibility to me. It was a duty that I accepted wholeheartedly and took seriously. My signing skills aside, I have often wondered whether I was chosen because my parents recognized that I was born a caretaker; or did I become a caretaker because I was chosen? I guess it doesn't matter, because it was all I knew. While I was aware that the world didn't only consist of deaf parents, I felt that my life was normal.

I was seven when my mother gave birth to my youngest brother, Jonny. Five children couldn't be managed financially on just my dad's salary, so my mom went to work when Jonny was around two years old; daycare was set up for him at a church across the highway from my elementary school. So, at the age of nine, I became a "latchkey kid." I wore a piece of yarn around my neck with the house key on it. There were times that I would leave my class to get my younger sister and brother from their classes; then we would walk across a major road to get my baby brother and walk about eight blocks home. Once home, we were to make sure that the house was picked up and dinner was ready by the time the *I Love Lucy* music came on the TV (our cue that my parents would soon be home). My childhood was full of responsibility. I knew of financial matters long before most children do. Financially, my parents never seemed to have enough, so I was often on the phone with creditors and bill collectors. I seemed to thrive on the responsibilities. No matter how it came to be, I grew up to be a nurturing caretaker, looking after everyone in my life.

Although we didn't have money for much, we always had our summer vacations. Most of them were spent going to Colorado for camping trips, taking Tim and Tammy along. On one of our earlier visits, I had decided that I would marry Tim. At the time, although I didn't consciously realize it, I think I saw a shy young boy who needed someone to help him through life. It was on the drive home, after a camping trip to Colorado, when I signed to my mom, "I will marry Tim someday."

"Don't be silly," my mom signed back. "You are too young to think about that now. You will have many boyfriends while you are growing up. No need to think about that now," she repeated. But I quietly knew that someday, the blond-haired, blue-eyed boy would be my husband.

One summer, my dad made an announcement. "We aren't going to Colorado this year. We are going to California," he signed. I was devastated. I loved California and visiting our family. But I wanted to see Tim. Vacation would not be the same, but vacation was vacation and I would enjoy it and have to make the best of it.

On the way home we stopped in Arizona to visit my dad's brother Milt, his wife Fran and my cousin Tracey. It was at this visit that I was made to realize that my life was not as normal as I thought it was. Milt and I were sitting at the table with my cousin sitting on his lap. He was lovingly poking fun at my Texan accent and then he said, "I see what you have to do for your parents and your family. Aunt Fran and I see how they treat you. It's not right; we want you to come and stay with us for the summer, to give you a break."

At the time, I was horrified! I began to think, why would he do this to his brother? Didn't he know? Didn't he know that, without me, there would be no one to take care of my parents? Who would watch the kids, clean, cook and field the creditors? Who would interpret for my parents when the store clerk didn't understand what they were asking for? Was he crazy?! Looking back, I see the care and compassion my uncle had for me. He did know, he knew too much, and he made me aware that what was expected of me on a day-to-day basis was not "normal."

The summer stay with Uncle Milt never happened; my dad put his foot down when approached by his brother about the subject: "No,

Tami can't stay. We have a lot to do this summer; we need her home." Whew! As inviting as a vacation sounded and felt, I wanted to be home, where I was needed. Although a new light had been shed on my responsibilities, I couldn't turn my back on them.

I've never complained about my childhood. There are those who ask why I was never "bitter" about the way I was raised and the loss of my childhood. My answer is this: I am who I am. Whether my childhood made me the person I am today or not, I don't know. I am a caretaker and I fit my childhood role perfectly. Again I ask, was I born a caretaker or was I nurtured to be one? I don't think I'll ever know. I embrace the deaf community and love the exposure I got from growing up in it. I learned life lessons from my childhood, and isn't that the way it's supposed to be? I learned to take responsibility seriously. I learned to care for others before myself. I learned that the world isn't fair, so you deal with it and make the most of it. I embrace the role given me and feel a sense of self-worth from it. Now why would I be bitter about any of that? I am who I am, and I love who I am.

In our early to mid-teens, Tim and I began writing letters to each other. It started after a summer visit from their family. The following Labor Day, my family and I went to Colorado for a visit. During this visit, Tim asked me to "go steady"; I gladly accepted and felt as though I was in love. After about a year of writing letters to each other, Tim and I were thrilled when we were told that my mom would be moving part of the family to Colorado. My parent's tumultuous marriage was crumbling, and I think Mom was looking for a way out. We moved to Colorado in 1978. Tim and I started dating right away; I was fifteen and he was seventeen.

My mom filed for divorce and at first it devastated all of us. We expected it, but I think the inner child in each of us didn't think it would really happen. It was an amicable divorce but still caused lasting pain in our family. My younger sister, Naomi, became pregnant at seventeen, in part due to this pain. She had a beautiful baby girl, Tina, whom we all adored.

Tim and I married in the fall of the year I graduated high school. Because we had a stable relationship and home, he and I had Tina a lot. We felt as though we were already a family. We loved each other, and it didn't matter to us then whether or not it was the "right" kind of love. We lived our life and I took care of my little family.

Soon after we married, I went to work at the family business that my father-in-law owned. Tim and I worked side by side. We never had a squabble between us, always doing what was expected. My relationship with my father-in-law, Melvin, deepened over the years and we have a bond that goes beyond the deaf connection. I will always call him my dad. I have learned so much from him. I was now his interpreter as well as one of the caretakers for his elderly mother, Granny, who lived on the property where the family business was located. I was still in the role of caretaker, exactly where I wanted and needed to be.

Life went on. We had three children: Brad, Mark and Amanda. It was after Amanda was a year old that I started to realize that I needed more from my marriage.

"Tim, I have an appointment with a psychiatrist on Monday," I said as we crawled into bed one night.

"A psychiatrist?" Tim's raised eyebrows showed his surprise.

"Yes, I feel like there's something wrong with me. I have three amazing children, we have a beautiful home and good jobs, but I feel like something is missing. I want to talk it over with someone to figure out what's wrong with me," I explained.

"What if they find out there was something bad in your childhood? Are you ready to face something like that?" he asked.

"I doubt that's it, but I'm prepared. I need to figure this out. There has to be a way to fix my feelings," I told him. We cuddled close—affection was never an issue between us—but I could feel his anxiety building.

"What if the psychiatrist tells you there's something wrong with me?" he asked.

"Then we'll deal with it if it comes up. But I think the problem lies deeper. I think there's more to just you being a problem or my childhood being a problem. I think it's something that I'm doing to myself, or not doing for myself. I don't know. I just know I need to stop being so unhappy," I told him.

"I don't think anyone would guess you are unhappy. You are always seem so happy and are always smiling. I guess that's why I'm puzzled. But if you need to do this, then you do," he assured me.

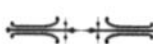

Monday morning's appointment with the psychiatrist came. The office was warm and inviting, decorated with antiques obviously collected on world travels. "What a life!" I thought to myself. I wanted a life like that. I longed to travel the world, with no responsibilities and no commitments, just travel. I yearned to travel with the love of my life at my side, sharing foreign places and food, making love in different cities all over the world, where famous and not so famous people had made love before us. What a wonderful life that would be, what a wonderful dream!

While Dr. Davidson took a seat, I sat fidgeting with my skirt as I tried to figure out where to start. "I feel like there is something wrong with me," I blurted out to the white-bearded, frail-looking man sitting across from me. As I tried to get comfortable on the couch it crinkled under my massive weight. Still a pretty young woman, I had ballooned to 280 pounds during the course of my marriage.

"I see," he said. "Perhaps we should start with introductions before we discuss why you feel you need to be here," he said in a comforting tone.

"I'm sorry; I've never been to a psychiatrist before. Not quite sure of how to do this, I guess."

"That's OK, just relax. Take a deep breath and let's start with who you are," he continued. His voice was warm and gentle; I trusted this stranger already.

After a deep breath and regrouping of myself, I said, "My name is Tami. I have been married for sixteen years to my childhood sweetheart. I have three children, work for my father-in-law and help take care of his mother. My parents, as well as my in-laws, are deaf. I interpret for them all when needed," I went on. "I have everything to be happy for, but I never feel happy. While I've never been thin, I've never been this heavy. I know I am eating for comfort. But I'm not happy finding comfort in food; I want to find comfort in my relationships with my children, family and, most importantly, with my husband."

"That's quite a start. You've already told me a lot in your first few minutes here. It's good that you recognize what's going on. Seems to me that what we need to do is figure out why it's going on this way," he told me. I was excited inside, as I would finally get to the bottom of this empty feeling that I'd had for so long. I would be able to be happy on the inside as well as on the outside. I was ready to "dig in" and do the work!

Over the next several months of therapy, I became painfully aware of my need to take care of others while ignoring my own needs. The reason that I found joy in working at the family business was because I was looking after Melvin, his business and extended family, as well as my own family. I was also taking care of Tim and his emotional needs to the detriment of my own.

I abruptly stopped therapy when I realized that my marriage might be based on a need to be taking care of everyone and not based on love. I was starting to suspect that I had married Tim because I could take care of him and his family. I had met the expectations of both of our families that we be married and had, perhaps, interpreted this as love for Tim. I didn't want to face the truth. I had too much invested in my family to even think about leaving Tim to find true love. Besides, who would want to love a 280-pound woman? More importantly, who would take care of everyone if I left?

Tim and I discussed separating and moving on a few times over the next few years. But neither of us carried through with the idea. "It would just be wrong," I told him one day. "We are supposed to be together. It's expected of us to be the 'perfect couple,'" I said, trying to convince Tim as well as myself.

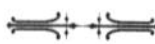

In the early part of the new century, business at the "shop" (as we called the family business) was on the decline. During this time, Tim's mother and grandmother passed away, and Tim left the shop to pursue his electrician's license, leaving me with fewer people to take care of. I did a lot of soul searching and came to the realization that I was a nurse. In every sense of the word, I was a nurse. I just needed to go to school to get the degree. The family and I decided that I would go to school while still continuing to run the business. I hired a wonderful young girl to help out at the shop. Even though there was a language barrier, she and Melvin formed a bond between them that made me feel at ease, because he was being taken care of while I was at school.

Things changed. I finished nursing school weighing over one hundred pounds less than when I had started; this was due to a gastric bypass I had undergone in December of 2004, just five months before graduation. I was feeling good about myself and knew that being a nurse is who I am. I now had fulfillment beyond my wildest dreams.

I was hired on the pediatric floor of the local hospital and soon realized that being a pediatric nurse is what I was born to be. I have a gift with all people, but especially with children. This magical skill came from somewhere else, I know. I don't own it; I am just the instrument. Parents raved about my skills and asked for me by name. My career was thriving, but my emotional life was still in crisis.

A few days after celebrating our twenty-fifth wedding anniversary, I was sitting on the couch with Tim and said, "I have an appointment on Wednesday with a family counselor to help our family get through a divorce."

"Divorce!" he exclaimed. "What?"

"You know as well as I do that our marriage isn't making either one of us happy," I continued. "We are different people who love each other, but not in the way that either one of us needs or wants. One of us has to put an end to this charade so we can be happy and find out what it is that we need or want in our lives."

Tim looked devastated. "Divorce—I can't imagine us really doing this," he said.

"We can talk it over some more tomorrow. I have to get to work now," I said, hoping to get out of the conversation for a little while.

Over the next three days, while working the night shift, Tim would call in tears, begging me to change my mind. Finally, on Tuesday, I succumbed to the pressure. Emotionally exhausted after three days of his pleading and fears, I finally said, "OK, we'll go to this counselor to seek marriage counseling instead of divorce counseling." I rationalized that twenty-five years of marriage warranted one last try to see if the problems could be fixed. I owed it to us and the children. But it was one of my children who, a few years before this day, had questioned my marriage.

Brad, my oldest, is truly one of the smartest people I have ever known. His IQ has been tested to be highly gifted, not a gift he received from me, but nonetheless, a gift. His intelligence is beyond his years, but his emotional intelligence at this time was lagging. Being away for his first semester of college, he seemed oblivious to the crisis at hand. The bond between a firstborn son and mother is beyond words, but he never picked up on my unhappiness, or perhaps I hid it well, for fear of disappointing him.

It was Mark, my second son, the man in my life since he was born, who seemed to know what was going on. His insight into people and their emotions rivals that of a well-trained psychiatrist. One day at lunch, almost four years before I decided to leave Tim, Mark said to me, "You know, Mom, I don't get it. I don't get your relationship with Dad. I know you love each other, but you're such different people. I don't understand why you're together."

"So what if we separated? How would you feel about that?" I asked him.

"I would be happy for you, because you could find the happiness you deserve. But I guess I would be sad and worried for Dad. It would be hard on him. He wouldn't know what to do with himself. I guess he'd be OK after a while, after he got things figured out. But he'd be in a tailspin to start," he explained.

Mark was thirteen when we had this discussion and showed rare empathy at an age when life is usually centered around oneself. With an insight into others that was way beyond his years, he must truly be an "old soul."

Amanda, my baby, would be hurt the most by the divorce. I had to think of her in all of this. I concluded, therefore, that marriage counseling was a good idea.

After some weeks of marriage counseling, it became painfully clear to me that Tim and I belonged together, but not as a married couple. This decision couldn't be made on my own; I needed help from God.

"He has always been my strength and my guidance. I will rely on him again to help me sort this out," I thought to myself.

I made arrangements with Tim so that I could take a long weekend to go to the mountains by myself; there, I could be lost in prayer and meditate on the decisions placed in front of me. After the weekend, I would have my answer. There was so much to consider, but this time, I had to consider myself and what I needed.

My children were older, except for Amanda, who was only ten. It would be hard on her, but I wanted her to know that happiness is ours for the taking, so that perhaps she would put her happiness first and be a better person in her relationships as well. I knew I needed to take care of myself now. I also believed that someday I would find the man of my dreams, the love of my life who wanted to take care of me as much as I wanted to take care of him. I would find true love, the kind that grows with nurturing from both parties. Now that I had made up my mind, the only thing left to do was to tell Tim.

CHAPTER 3

THE NIGHTMARE BEGINS

Once settled in Speicher, Germany, Gaye missed the children and grandchildren terribly. She seemed to be feeling sad a lot. "I can't wait to get back to Colorado to see the kids," she told Eric as they booked their plane tickets. Rix was getting married and they were headed home for the wedding.

"We haven't been gone that long, Gaye," Eric said.

"Yes, but I've been feeling blue so much lately, and I think this is just the ticket to get me feeling better. I'll get my 'kid fix' then be ready to come back here to do all the sightseeing you've been promising me."

The trip back home was wonderful. Gaye and Eric arrived at the rehearsal dinner the night before the wedding. They were excited to see their children, grandsons and daughter-in-law to be, Emily—and to spend time with the newest addition to the family, whom they hadn't met. "Mom, Dad, this is Megan." Rix introduced them to a smiling little girl with brown hair. Megan was Emily's daughter from a previous relationship.

"It's just like your dad and me. When we met, I had Mel," Gaye told her son. "It's so nice to meet you, Megan" she said as she hugged her new granddaughter.

On the return flight to Europe, Gaye felt less depressed than she had been. "I must have been missing the kids," she thought to herself. "I should be fine now. We've got so much to see when we get home, I'm so excited!"

⁂

But the depression didn't stop; it only got worse after their return. Gaye was crying all the time—not acting like herself—in spite of the wonderful experiences of traveling to so many amazing places. It seemed that nothing lifted her spirits. She also became concerned about her memory. She felt as though she couldn't remember the simplest of tasks. She wanted desperately to drive, so that she could go on day trips while Eric was at work. But for some reason, she couldn't pass the driving test, despite taking it five times. The forgetfulness and frustrations only made her depression worse. She became more and more concerned about her own behavior and decided to address the issue with Eric.

This particular morning they were heading to Trier, a German city about thirty miles away from where they were living. Eric had taken the day off and they were, originally, going to travel to Belgium for the weekend. But, for some reason, Eric abruptly cancelled the trip with no explanation to her as to why. But he promised to take her to their favorite coffee shop and to do some shopping along the Mosel. She would talk to him there.

Once seated at the coffee shop, Gaye began to discuss her concerns. "Eric, there's something wrong with me. I cry at the slightest things. Sometime yesterday, I put the aluminum foil in the refrigerator and when I found it there later, it made me cry. I think I should see a doctor. I wonder if I'm depressed," she told him.

"Do you think that's it?" Eric asked, concerned. "I've noticed it too. You seem a bit withdrawn, not yourself. I thought that perhaps it's because we've been traveling so much and entertaining a lot. With first your parents and then mine coming out to stay with us, I figured that perhaps you were just exhausted from it all. That's why I called off the trip to Belgium today; I wanted us to take a rest. I thought that maybe if you rest up and relax, you might feel better," he told her.

"Maybe," she said, "but I think I should see a doctor. Sometimes I find myself crying, but I don't know why and I don't remember starting to cry. Then, all of a sudden, I'll realize I've been crying for a long time, because of my face is drenched in tears, my nose is running and my eyes are red and swollen. It's a weird feeling. It's like waking up from a dream, crying, but I was never asleep and never had the dream. It's so scary. I suppose it could have something to do with depression and being tired of traveling. Or I've even thought maybe it was menopause. I've talked to Madlyn on the phone about my symptoms and she thinks it's menopause, because she's having some of the same symptoms."

Gaye and her sister-in-law, Madlyn, who was married to Eric's brother, Don, were of the same age and very close. Gaye always felt that if she ever needed to talk to someone, she could always count on Madlyn. "But whatever it is, I know it's something and I want to figure this out soon," she continued. "I hate this feeling of being lost in my own body, not being able to find my way."

"Then you're right, you need to see a doctor," Eric agreed. "You call on Monday to make an appointment. I'll bet you and Madlyn are right, I'll bet its menopause. I think you might be able to take medication for that. Then you'll be feeling better in no time," he assured her.

They spent the weekend just relaxing and trying to catch up on rest. But Eric noticed something was wrong. Gaye seemed to forget the simplest things. She even looked different to him—her eyes appeared as if she were lost. She looked the same way as she described herself: "I feel like I'm lost in my body and I can't find my way." Perhaps she was looking for herself.

She seemed to have forgotten how to quilt. She thought she was quilting correctly, but Eric knew his wife's work, and what she was doing now was not it. Eric was alarmed but had confidence that the doctor would be able to treat this illness, whatever it was.

What Gaye didn't share with Eric that day was that she feared she had Alzheimer's. She did, however, share the idea while on the phone with her sister-in-law a few days later. "Madlyn, I'm worried I have Alzheimer's. I'm so forgetful and keep putting things in weird places and finding them later. I can't pass the driving test here and sometimes I can't even dial the phone to call someone. I feel depressed and cry all the time. I'm so afraid, Madlyn. I can't bear the thought of having the same disease that took my grandmother away. I can't bear the thought of wasting away like that, with everyone having to suffer through watching me. It was a terrible thing to have to watch, and I don't want anyone ever having to see me like that. Oh Madlyn, tell me it's not Alzheimer's," Gaye pleaded as her voice faltered and she fought back tears.

"Gaye! Of course it's not! You're a young woman. Way too young to get Alzheimer's. Don't even think about it. You're just thinking about it because it's been such a fear of yours. Ever since I met you, you've talked about how you're afraid of getting it," Madlyn tried to console her. "It's just your fear taking over your mind now. It's not Alzheimer's! Did your grandmother cry a lot or seem depressed like you do?" she asked.

"Not that I remember," she said, feeling a small flicker of hope.

"See, you're more than likely depressed from menopause. I've been reading a lot about it, because I think I'm having a lot of forgetfulness as well. Menopause causes forgetfulness, depression and lots of other things. The crying and your age both tell me that it's not Alzheimer's. Please don't worry about it for now. You'll get to the bottom of this after you see the doctor. He'll get it figured out and get you on medication. You'll see," she tried to reassure her.

Gaye began to think like Madlyn. Surely she was too young to have Alzheimer's, wasn't she? She pushed the thought out of her mind.

⟡

Monday morning, Gaye called Eric at work. "I've got an appointment tomorrow morning at nine. Can you take me?" she asked him. "I'm not quite sure I could find the clinic on base." She was painfully aware that she couldn't drive there because she might forget how.

"Sure, I'll let my boss know I'll be in late tomorrow," he told her. "I'm glad you got in so soon. The sooner we figure out what's going on and get you treated, the better," he told her.

The next morning, the trip to the doctor was uneventful. He was sure it was "empty nest syndrome," which he felt was heightened by her leaving the family so far behind in the United States. He explained that depression can lead to forgetfulness. He drew some labs to check to see if she was menopausal and prescribed an antidepressant to see if it would help.

A phone call from the doctor a few days later confirmed that Gaye was not menopausal. "Hello Mrs. Reeves, this is Dr. Chacon; I received the results from your blood work, and it all looks normal. Your FSH is within range, so you are not menopausal or even pre-menopausal," he explained. "I feel strongly that you are experiencing depression. Let's continue with the plan of treatment with the medication. Unless things get worse, I'd like to see you in a month to determine if there are any changes."

"Well, I guess it's good that my labs were normal. But disappointing too; I was so hoping that it was menopause. But if you're pretty sure it's depression. I'll keep taking the medication," Gaye assured him.

"Now remember, as I told you in here in the office, it takes a while for the medication to take effect. So be faithful and take it as I prescribed and I'll see you next month," he told her.

That night, Eric arrived home from work and found the house to be unusually dark when he entered. "Gaye? Gaye, are you home?" he seemed to be shouting at emptiness. He listened for a moment and heard whimpering coming from the spare bedroom. As he entered, he found her face down on the bed crying. “Gaye, are you OK?” he said as he picked her up to face him.

“Yes, of course I’m OK. Why do you ask?” she said, smiling, but her eyes were red and swollen as tears streamed down her face.

“You’re...you’re crying. Are you OK?” he asked again.

“I’m not crying. I was just getting ready to get, to get…Oh brother! I forgot what I came into this room to get!” she exclaimed with frustration on her face.

“Gaye, your face looks as if you’ve been crying for hours. Here, look in the mirror,” he said as he led her to the mirror in the hall.

“Oh my goodness! You’re right; I do look like I’ve been crying for a while. See, Eric, this is what I mean! I don’t even remember coming into this room, much less starting to cry. I’m so frightened! What is wrong with me?” she shouted.

“Have you heard from the doctor yet, about the labs?” he asked her.

“Yes, he called today.” Gaye repeated what the doctor had told her. One thing, she recalled, was discouraging: “He said that it takes a while for the medication to work. I thought I’d take the pills and be better right away,” she told him.

“Gaye, he explained to us in his office that it takes a while for an antidepressant to work. Don’t you remember?” he asked.

“No, I don’t remember him explaining anything to me in the office about the medication, except that I should take it twice a day,” she said.

Fear took hold of Eric. Gaye had even asked the doctor specific questions about the medication during the visit, he thought to himself. Why didn’t she remember that? She had asked about how long it would take for it to work, how often to take it, and what side effects it might have; now she doesn’t remember the conversation at all. He tried to console himself with the thought that maybe the medication would work quicker than they expected and she would be feeling better soon.

Gaye looked up at Eric. "What are you thinking?" she asked.

"That I'm hungry and we need to get dinner," he lied to her.

"Oh! Dinner! I forgot about getting dinner. What time is it?" she asked.

"It's all right; let's go warm up that left over soup. Soup sounds good," he said as they headed downstairs. As he watched her move around the kitchen, he struggled with the fear that had taken hold of him. What if she was really, really sick? What if there is something that the doctor hasn't thought of? He shook his head as if to fend off the thought that was trying to enter.

As they finished their soup, Gaye looked at Eric. "What do you think this is?" she asked, almost afraid to hear what he would reply.

"I don't know, but Dr. Chacon is a good doctor. I'm sure if the medication doesn't work, he'll figure it out. Gaye, you have to stop worrying so much. Let's give the medicine a chance to work," he urged.

"It's just the strangest feeling in the world to realize that I keep forgetting that I'm crying. And I'm forgetting so much lately, so much that I wonder what else it could be. It scares me to death to think about it. I'm so afraid of what might be wrong with me!" She began to sob.

He wrapped his arms around her and held her tight. The thought he had shoved away earlier tried to reenter his mind and, again, he pushed it away. "Promise me you will stop worrying. I'm sure if Dr. Chacon thought it was something more serious, then he would have run more tests. Apparently, he doesn't, so we shouldn't jump to conclusions. Dr. Chacon was sure it was depression. It just makes sense—we've left the children far away. But for now, let's not worry. OK?" he pleaded.

"Yes, you're right. I'll not worry about it anymore," she said. "Oh dear, it's getting late. I had better fix dinner." She jumped up.

"It's OK, Gaye," Eric said, trying not to be alarmed that she had forgotten in fifteen minutes that they had just eaten. "Let's just go for a walk. It's such a nice evening. Let's just go for a walk."

The depression continued. The medication had not alleviated Gaye's symptoms and Dr. Chacon sent her to another doctor for a second opinion. Dr. Lewis agreed with Dr. Chacon's diagnosis of depression and put her on a different antidepressant.

The car was silent as they drove down the winding roads back to their home in the town of Speicher. "Can I drive?" Gaye asked Eric, breaking the silence.

"Right now?" he asked.

"Yes, I haven't driven in such a long time. And it's such a beautiful day. Would you mind?" she asked.

"Of course not," he told her as he pulled the car over and stopped.

Gaye sat in the driver's seat and pressed the gas pedal. "Put your seat belt on first," Eric reminded her.

"Oh yes, thank you," she said as she reached for her seat belt and snapped it. "OK, now..." She fumbled with the gear shift and pressed the gas pedal again.

The engine revved loudly, "No Gaye, not the gas pedal, the brake pedal, and don't forget the clutch," he told her.

"Yes, of course." She pressed the gas pedal again revving the car even louder.

"Gaye, that's the gas pedal. You need to press the brake pedal and the clutch, until you can shift the car into drive," he told her.

"I know how to drive a car," she snapped at him. After fifteen agonizing minutes, Gaye finally managed to get the car to lunge twenty feet. "Which one is the gas pedal, again? I'm not quite understanding this," she said to him in desperation.

Eric spent the next twenty-five minutes trying to help her remember how to drive. It was fruitless, as she couldn't grasp the concept. They finally agreed to give up and they switched back. There were no words between them the rest of the way home. Eric was deep in thought. "She can't even drive a car anymore...What is this? What is taking over my wife's mind like this?" As he drove home on "auto pilot" he made a decision. When they pulled into the driveway of their home, he told Gaye, "We're going back to the States."

"What? Are they sending you back home?" she asked.

"No, I'm going to get it all arranged. We are going back to the States to find someone who can figure out what is going on with you. We need to fix this before it can't be fixed," he told her.

"I think that's a wonderful idea! When do we go?" she asked, excited.

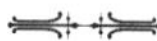

Eric was working for the military as a civilian; he was able to transfer to another position "stateside" due to his wife's medical necessity. Packing, cleaning, kenneling two dogs, and making all the arrangements were weighing heavily on them. They were fortunate to have had Gaye's mother, Ila, come to help them, but they were still exhausted. Somehow they got through it all, and within two weeks, they were on flight to Chicago, where they would change to a plane bound for Colorado Springs. As their plane landed in Chicago, Gaye was smiling.

"What are you smiling at?" Eric asked her.

"We're almost home! We'll get to see the kids and grand kids. More importantly, we are going to find a doctor to fix me," she said.

"Absolutely! We will get this resolved; then once you're better, we'll go back to Germany," he told her.

"Yes! That sounds perfect," she said.

They departed the plane. Once inside the terminal, Eric glanced up at a monitor to see which concourse they needed to head to. Gaye disappeared. Frantically looking around, Eric called her name. But she didn't answer and he couldn't see her. Just as he was going to find someone to help him, he spotted her standing at a window. "Gaye!

Where have you been? I've been looking for you," he said, relieved at finding her.

"I thought you wanted me to stand here," she answered.

"Let's go," he said, "our concourse is over here." They walked over to a long line that was demarcated by guide ropes and poles. As they stood in line, Eric felt as though Gaye wasn't herself and decided he couldn't take his eyes off her, so he positioned himself behind her with their carry-on luggage. As they approached the end of the line, the guide rope was in front of Gaye, indicating that she should turn right. Eric noticed her standing still, as if she didn't know what to do next.

"Keep going," Eric told her.

"Going where? There's this rope here, so I can't go anywhere," she told him.

Eric gently took her shoulder and turned her in the direction of the guide rope, but apparently she was confused. "My God! She doesn't even understand to keep moving to the right; the rope made her stop!" Eric thought to himself. "This is getting worse right in front of my eyes! What is this monster? What has taken over my wife?"

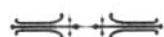

After a brief stay at Mel's house, their new home was completed and they moved in. Gaye announced to Eric one day over breakfast, "I want to plant bleeding hearts all around the backyard, like the ones we used to have."

"Sure, whatever you want. Once the trees are planted and the landscaping is done, we'll plant hundreds of them," he assured her.

It wasn't long before Eric found a doctor who could see Gaye right away, and he made an appointment for the following week. It was excruciating being at work all day and worrying about Gaye. When he was home, he worried about her enough, but at work he wasn't sure what she was doing, or if she was OK. He would call her several times a day to check on her. Finally, the day of the appointment came.

After a detailed and lengthy history was given to Dr. Noble, he promptly sent Gaye to a neurologist. They arrived in the neurologist's office a few days later for the appointment. It was a comfortable office. "Thick plush chairs that one could curl up and read a book in," Gaye thought. A soft ticktock from an old clock on the wall was soothing to them both. They were anxious about being there and the surroundings helped calm them.

Then a nurse called them into the doctor's office. "Stanley Mayfield, PhD" read the plaque on his desk. They seated themselves in the two chairs in front of the doctor's desk. The office was decorated in the same comfortable style as the waiting room; a large bookcase filled with books stood behind the doctor's desk. There was a window that faced north; it was a beautiful early-spring morning in 2003.

After a few moments the door opened behind them and in walked a thin man with a graying beard and balding head. His eyes were lively behind his glasses; he removed his jacket and placed it on the coat rack behind the door. He approached Gaye. "Hello, I'm Dr. Mayfield," he said as he extended his hand to Gaye.

"I'm Gaye Reeves," she replied as she shook his hand. "This is my husband, Eric," she said.

"Nice to meet you both. I spoke with Dr. Noble yesterday and we both felt we needed to be a bit aggressive in trying to pinpoint a diagnosis," he explained. "Thank you for coming so quickly. Now tell me, in your own words, about your symptoms," he said as he looked at Gaye.

They discussed the symptoms that Gaye identified. She was silently horrified when Eric began adding symptoms that he had observed that she was not aware of—things she didn't know she was doing or not doing or forgetting. They both went on to explain the medications and diagnoses that were her history over the past few months. After a few questions of his own, Dr. Mayfield then ordered an MRI, EEG, blood work and a spinal tap, "to cover everything," he explained to them.

"If these tests all prove to be normal, we'll take the next step, a full neuropsychological evaluation," he told them. The arrangements were all made; the tests would start in a couple of days and he would call to set up the next appointment, depending on what was needed.

"The tests were all normal," Dr. Mayfield told Eric over the phone a week later. "I'm not finding anything that points to a diagnosis. Gaye is healthy, according to all the tests we've run."

"That's both disappointing and good, I guess," Eric confided leaning back on his chair, rubbing his forehead. "We were both hoping that something would come up that could be fixed," he told the doctor.

"Yes, I was too. The next step is the neuropsych testing. I have availability on Tuesday at nine—can you and Gaye be here?" he asked. Eric assured him they could.

Tuesday morning, Eric and Gaye prepared to go to Dr. Mayfield's office. "Eric, I can't remember, where we are going today?" Gaye asked her husband.

She had asked several times already. He patiently reminded her, "We're going to see Dr. Mayfield to finish up the testing."

Once in the office, Gaye and Eric were escorted to a room that resembled a classroom, and the testing began. After some preliminary verbal tests, Dr. Mayfield said, "Gaye, I'm going to read a sentence to you and I want you to repeat it. Then I need you to remember it, because I'm going to ask you to say it again at the end of the testing. OK?"

Gaye nodded.

"There is a store at the corner of Tejon and Pikes Peak that sells mittens," he stated. "Now you repeat the sentence, Gaye."

"There is a store at the corner of...What street?" she asked the doctor.

"Tejon and Pikes Peak," he reminded her.

"Oh yes, there is a store at the corner of Tejon and Pikes Peak," she repeated.

"That sells mittens," he reminded her.

"Oh, they do?" she asked.

"Gaye, I want you to repeat the sentence, 'There is a store at the corner of Tejon and Pikes Peak that sells mittens,'" he told her again, as he looked up from taking notes.

"There is a store at the corner of Tejon and Pikes Peak that sells... something." Gaye looked at Eric. "Oh! Mittens! There is a store at the corner of Tejon and Pikes Peak that sells mittens!" Gaye said, excited that she had repeated the sentence exactly as Dr. Mayfield had requested.

"OK, that's fine. Now that you remember that sentence, I'm going to ask you for it again later."

She nodded.

Now let's move on to another test. With each test, Gaye struggled to complete the task that was given to her; at times it seemed as though she didn't understand what was being asked, much less completing the task correctly. Eric tried to offer help, but the doctor reminded him that Gaye had to complete the tests on her own.

It was hard for Eric to not help his wife; he had done so for their entire marriage. He had always had to help her with one thing or another, ever since he could remember. But now, he had to sit back and let her fumble through the directions and the task. He watched as Gaye continued to struggle. With some of the tasks, she seemed to be confident that she was completing them correctly; but between understanding a task and completing it, there was information lost in the translation from brain to hand and the task would be completed wrong.

Eric watched in horror as the "clock test" was presented to her. "Gaye," Dr. Mayfield said, "now I want you to draw me a clock with the time set at 3:00."

"Sure," she said as she picked up the pencil and moved it to the paper. She placed the point of the pencil on the paper and began to draw. The pencil seemed to have a mind of its own; Gaye tried to make it move into what Eric assumed was a round circle like the face of a clock, but the pencil wouldn't seem to cooperate. "What's wrong with this pencil?" she wondered out loud, as she looked up at Eric. He offered to help her, but the doctor again reminded him that she had to complete the task herself. After five minutes of letting her struggle, Dr. Mayfield ended her agony by telling her that it was OK, that the test was over.

"Gaye, do you remember the sentence I told you when we first started?" he asked.

"Oh, yes...um, something about a kitten?"

CHAPTER 4

THE DIAGNOSIS

Eric knew what was going to happen next. But there was nothing he could do but wait patiently for the outcome that would change his and Gaye's lives forever.

Dr. Mayfield had explained that he needed a few moments to put all the test results together and asked them to wait while he analyzed the data. Sitting in the office, Eric felt a fear that he had never experienced before. Witnessing Gaye not able to draw the circle of the clock, when she was such a talented painter, made him think the worst. But again, he shook his head to keep the demon word out of his mind.

A few moments later, Dr. Mayfield came in behind them and took his seat behind his desk. "I believe I have a probable diagnosis. I'm so sorry, it's very difficult to tell such a young, able-bodied woman this, but you have probable early-onset Alzheimer's" he explained.

"Probable?" Eric asked with a tremor in his voice, trying to catch his breath.

"We say 'probable' because there is only one way to confirm Alzheimer's and that's postmortem. Your wife has all the signs of early-onset Alzheimer's," he said solemnly.

"Alzheimer's," Gaye said through tears. "I'm only forty-nine. That's not old enough to have Alzheimer's, is it?" she managed to ask him.

"All the scans and tests we did last week were to rule out any other brain event that it could have been. The testing today confirms my suspicions that you have Alzheimer's, Gaye. I'm so sorry," he said.

"Is there anything we can do?" Eric asked. "I've heard about medications that can help."

"We'll start you on medication right away," he said as he turned back to Gaye. "It can't cure the disease, but it has been found to help slow down the progression and sometimes even improve functioning to a point," the doctor said as he took out his prescription pad.

Eric wrapped his arms around Gaye and told her, "See, he's going to give us a prescription. It'll help, you'll see. You'll start getting better. We'll just make sure you take the medicine every day, OK?"

"Yes, I'll take the medicine and I'll get better," she said, wiping her tears.

The drive home was quiet. Eric was deep in thought about how to take care of his wife and gripped by fear of how the disease would progress. He looked over at Gaye; she seemed to be lost in another world, oblivious to the heinous death sentence that she had just received. Perhaps it was better for her to be in that world right now. "What do we do?" he wondered and thought of Mel.

"Gaye," Eric finally broke the silence. "We need to tell the kids. Mel knew we were having the testing done; she'll want to know what we found out."

"Yes, I was just thinking about that. I can call her when I get home," she told him.

"No, we can tell her when we go to Pueblo with her birthday present. We were going to visit her next weekend anyway; we'll tell her then," he suggested.

They arrived at Mel's house early Saturday morning. They exchanged hugs and pleasantries, and Mel opened her gift. "Thanks Mom and Dad, how did you know I needed a new coffeemaker?" she said coyly to her parents. She had given her parents the hint when, a few weeks before, they'd asked her what she wanted for her birthday.

Noticing a difference in her mom's demeanor, as well as in her eyes, Mel soon asked, "So, Mom, last I heard, your tests had all come back normal. When do we go on to the neuropsychological evaluation? Isn't that the next step?"

As they all took a seat, Eric blurted it out: "Your mother has Alzheimer's." There it was—the nasty ugly word that, for so many months, Eric had tried to keep out of his mind. Now it invaded not only his mind but also his life. The silence could have been cut with a knife.

"Alzheimer's?" Mel asked more in shock at the way it was presented than in disbelief of the diagnosis.

"Yes, well, they call it 'probable early-onset Alzheimer's,' because nothing else could be found and the true definitive diagnosis can only come postmortem by autopsy. But the doctor has prescribed a new medication that should help. Mom has started taking it already," Eric reassured her.

Mel's mind was reeling from the news. She looked to her husband, Jamie, for what to say next. "Have you told Rix?" Mel asked.

"No, not yet. Maybe you could tell him," her father answered.

Then Eric changed the subject. "Oh, we leave for California next Friday. We are going to visit Deanna and Jack." (Eric's sister and her husband lived in the San Francisco area.) "Then we'll drive up the coast to the Napa Valley, do some wine tasting, then over to Grandma's in Idaho Falls. It will be a wonderful trip!"

"Your dad and I will have such a wonderful vacation," Gaye added.

"California? Are you still going" Mel asked, stammering over her words and still trying to process the diagnosis.

"Yes, we've been planning this for such a long time. I can't wait to go," her mother exclaimed.

"Good, good, I'm glad you're going." Mel finally got the words out. Eric then abruptly stood and announced that they needed to go home. Mel and her family walked her parents to their car. They all said their good-byes and Eric and Gaye left for home.

Mel was shaking as she closed the door. Her husband looked into his wife's eyes. "Mel, are you OK?" Jamie asked as he reached out his arms to try and comfort his wife.

"Yes, but hearing such a horrendous diagnosis that bluntly is so shocking. Oh Jamie! My mom has Alzheimer's! And she's not even fifty yet. What's going to become of her? It's such a terrible disease! My poor dad! I'd better call and tell Rix. I can't believe they are still going to California! What is my dad thinking?" she said with her mind racing.

"They need to do what they can, while they can," Jamie reminded her. "And you need to slow down. Sit down and take a deep breath. I'll get you a glass of water. Sit here," he said as he led her to the couch in the family room.

"Alzheimer's," repeated Mel. "It's such a nasty word," she told her husband.

"I know it is. I'm so sorry, I'm so sorry that your mom is sick," he said as he handed her the water. She, robotically, put the glass on the coffee table.

"I've got to call Rix. My dad wants me to call him. I don't know how he's going to take this," she said after taking a few deep breaths.

Mel walked to the phone and began to dial. "How do I tell him?" she wondered as she heard the phone ring through the receiver.

After a couple of attempts at trying to reach her brother, Mel finally got Rix on the phone. "Rix, Mom and Dad were here today for my birthday. They told us they have a diagnosis for what Mom has," Mel started. Rix, was used to getting family news, good or bad, this way, via Mel. Melanie was the older of the two and was also the main information source when it came to family plans, news, and so on.

"OK, so what is it?" Rix's voice had a catch in it, as if he were almost afraid to ask.

"Alzheimer's—Mom has early-onset Alzheimer's," she told him. "Well, probable early-onset Alzheimer's," she added.

After a few moments of silence, Rix asked, "What's probable early-onset Alzheimer's?" Rix asked.

Mel explained the use of the term *probable* and added, "It's 'early-onset' because of how young she is. They have Mom taking some kind of pill that should slow the progression," she explained.

"But there's no cure. Rix, Mom will die of this! Just like her grandmother did. Mom was always afraid she would end up with it. Rix, we're too young to lose our mom, and she's too young to have this. This is all so unfair," she exclaimed as she broke into tears.

Even through her despair, she could hear the pain in her brother's voice on the other end of the line. Obviously, he was fighting his own pain as he tried to comfort her. "It's OK, Mel. What do you know about early-onset Alzheimer's?" he asked her.

"I've done a bit of reading about Alzheimer's because I was worried that Mom might have it. It's a horrible disease, Rix. It's horrible!" she said with tears burning her eyes.

"How much time does she have? What do we do? Besides Mom taking the medication, is there anything else we should be doing?" Rix asked.

"I don't know. There's not much we can do. Just keep her comfortable until she passes away—who knows when that will be. The disease doesn't usually kill the person; they usually die from pneumonia or something else that's caused by being incapacitated by the disease. I don't know how long we have left with our mom, Rix. But I know what I'm thinking" she told her brother.

"What's that?" he asked.

"That we need to have a big family Christmas this year. Everyone has to come, no ifs, ands or buts…Everyone has to come! It could be the last year Mom even knows what Christmas is, or who any of us are," she said, feeling fear as the words came from her mouth.

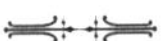

Packing for the trip was challenging. Gaye would pack items and not remember if she had done so or not and would go searching for the same items she had just packed. But the mood was good. Eric wasn't going to let anything ruin what might be their last vacation together. As they left the house, their spirits were high.

The drive proved to be long and painful. Every few hours Gaye would ask, "What did the doctor say I had again?"

Eric would have to explain, "Alzheimer's. They say you have Alzheimer's".

"What? Alzheimer's?! No, not Alzheimer's! Eric, I'm so afraid!" she would say between sobs.

The pain was too unbearable. Eric decided that he couldn't answer the question again and witness her grief each time she realized the diagnosis. The next time Gaye asked, he merely replied, "You just have to take that pill I give you. The doctor says it will make you better." It was a partial truth, but Eric knew he couldn't let Gaye suffer anymore than she was going to have to already.

The visit to Eric's sister's house was enjoyable, but bittersweet because everyone knew. Deanna and Jack witnessed, firsthand, the memory loss and changes in Gaye; they were saddened that such a young, attractive woman could be stricken with such a horrific disease.

The drive through Napa was beautiful. Eric kept reassuring Gaye that "the pill will help" every time Gaye asked about her diagnosis. As they neared their next destination, Gaye's mother's house in Idaho

Falls, they stopped for lunch. It was when they got back to the car that Gaye broke down. She seemed to have had a moment when she realized what her diagnosis was.

"Eric! Alzheimer's! No, no, not Alzheimer's!" Her sobbing seemed to go on forever. Eric tried as best he could to comfort his wife. But how does one comfort someone who has had such a death sentence placed on them? Eric's tears flowed—how would he cope with this? How, when things get worse, would he care for Gaye? What would their life be like? What was in store for them? More importantly, all Eric could do was think, "Poor Gaye, she doesn't deserve this."

A few weeks after Eric and Gaye returned home, Melanie called her dad up. "Dad! We're going to have a great big family Christmas! I am telling everyone that they *have* to come, no question about it! This may be the last Christmas that Mom will be 'here.' I've told everyone and there is plenty of time for them all to make arrangements. We'll have it at your place. Everyone will come. It's going to be great!"

The truth set in, as Eric listened to his daughter talking excitedly about the plans. Mel was right—no one really knew how long Gaye would be "here." No one knew how long it would be before her memory was completely gone. No one knew how long it would take before her body would finally be defeated by this terrible disease. What do we do until then, he wondered...until what? "I can't think about the 'what,'" he muttered to himself. "I have to stay in the here and now to make the most of it for Gaye. Here and now," he thought.

"That's wonderful," Eric told his daughter, trying to sound excited. "We'll have a great big family Christmas. Mom will love it!"

Life went on, and Gaye began to grow increasingly frustrated at trying to paint. She always took such joy in creating Christmas gifts for her family. This year, she wanted to paint Santas for her family.

As she attempted her first project, it seemed as though her hands wouldn't obey what her mind was demanding of them.

It was excruciating for Eric to watch, and he wondered what Gaye must be feeling inside. Did she even realize that her once-skilled hands, which could paint a Santa with such precision—beautifully, with every detail meticulously accurate—now seemed to have lost their skill? Now Gaye barely managed getting the paint on the board, slurs of colors running together. "Is that how her mind is working?" Eric would wonder to himself.

Gaye's increasing frustration led her to finally give up. Her hands stilled, she began wandering. She'd wander the house incessantly, as if she were looking for something she'd misplaced.

During the day, while Eric was at work, Gaye would be alone. Because she wouldn't answer the phone, Eric would have to come home from work, sometimes twice a day, just to check on her, for fear she was injured or, worse, that she had wandered outside and become lost. There were times when Gaye would be on the phone with Eric, put the phone down, then go looking for him, thinking she was talking to him in person, in the house. She would wander through the rooms, calling "Eric..." He'd come home to find the phone on the counter and Gaye still prowling the house, calling his name.

Eventually Eric had to change the stovetop from gas to electric, fearing that Gaye would burn herself or start a fire. Gaye would call Eric and ask how to make her lunch. "Eric, there's an instant cup of noodles and a cup of water on the counter. I am hungry, how do I cook it again?" she'd call to ask him.

He'd have to explain, "Yes, that's for your lunch. Open it up and pour the water in it." She followed his instructions. "Now put the top back on and put it in the top oven, not the bottom one," he continued.

"OK, it's in there; now what am I supposed to do?" she'd ask.

"Push the two, then the three and the zero, then hit the green 'start' button," he'd explain. Finally, he'd hear the whir of the microwave and know that her lunch was cooking. Sometimes, Eric wouldn't hear the microwave running and, only after a series of questions, would figure out that Gaye had forgotten to shut the microwave door or to push start. Some days were better, though, and she needed little or no instruction. Eric lived for those days; he could get glimpses of *his* Gaye on those days. On bad days, he felt as though he were living with a stranger. He likened it to how she must have felt when she first became aware of the symptoms in Germany, aware of "being lost in my own body."

Christmas came. *Everyone* made it. Melanie was successful in getting the whole family to come to the festivities. Mel, Rix and Eric were determined to make it a Merry Christmas, and it was, for the most part. Everyone enjoyed themselves, but in the back of everyone's thoughts, there was the ache of knowing what had brought about the reunion. But an announcement by Rix and Emily added joy to the festivities—they were expecting! It was welcome and exciting news in the midst of all the sadness.

The next August, Brian Ray Reeves was born. Eric and Gaye traveled to Longmont, in northern Colorado, to see their new grandson. Everyone was so happy, and Gaye seemed to be in heaven, holding her baby grandson, who was the spitting image of his father. "He looks just like you when you were born," she told Rix.

It warmed Rix's heart to know that his mom still had that memory. "Yeah, that's what everyone keeps saying. Megan is crazy about him, quite the little mamma to him already," he told his mother.

"I'm so happy for you and Emily," she exclaimed.

On their way home, Eric broke the silence of the drive. "What a great day! Little Brian is healthy and—you're right—he looks just like Rix," he said to Gaye.

"Who's Brian?" she asked Eric with a puzzled look on her face.

"Rix's son, the baby we just saw, Gaye," he tried to explain.

"Whose baby?" she asked.

"Rix, our son. He and Emily just had a baby they named Brian. We were just there. You said he looks just like Rix when he was born." He tried to jar her memory.

"I didn't see the baby; can I see the baby?" she asked.

Defeated, Eric replied, "Yes, Gaye, we'll go see the baby soon. I promise".

Time moved on. Some days Eric came home twice a day to check on Gaye; other days it was three times. It was wearing on him, everyone knew it. Then it was suggested to him that he hire a home health nurse to help take care of Gaye. What a relief that would be!

Annie, a niece of Madlyn's, was hired for the job. Prior to this, Gaye was having more bad days then good and had started developing a mistrust of everything and everyone, even Eric. On the first day, it was apparent that Gaye didn't trust this woman who was in her home. She yelled and screamed at her until she finally left the house.

"Eric, this is Annie," said a scared sounding voice as he picked up the phone. "I can't stay here anymore today. Gaye thinks I'm trying to steal her things and started swearing at me and made me leave. I'm afraid to go back in there—she's awful mad," she told him.

"I'm sure she'll be OK; I'll be home in a couple of hours. Can you come back again tomorrow?" he asked her.

"We can try it again; maybe after being around me a bit today, she'll be a little more relaxed around me tomorrow. I'll give it a try," she told him.

The next morning, Eric decided to stay for a time with Gaye while Annie was there. Gaye kept asking Eric who the woman was and why she was in her house. He finally, or so he thought, convinced her that it was OK for Annie to be there—that she was there to help Gaye do whatever she needed. She seemed to accept the idea of having a "helper," and Eric breathed a sigh of relief; he would have help for Gaye and wouldn't need to worry while he was at work.

But the situation only lasted a couple of weeks. One day Eric received a phone call and heard the now-familiar voice: "Eric, this isn't going to work. I can't stay with Gaye anymore; she thinks I'm after her for something. She's calling me names, yelling at me, and I just can't stay; she doesn't want me here," Annie said with a defeated voice.

"I understand," Eric consoled her. "I know, I know, and it's OK, Annie. Thanks for everything you've done. I'll come home."

"Maybe it's time for her to be in an Alzheimer's unit, Eric," she offered. "There are some really nice places here in the Springs. Maybe you could look into one."

Eric refused to entertain the idea—that would just be to admit defeat, and he wasn't ready to give up. On his way home, he called Mel. "Mel, Annie said she can't take care of Mom anymore. I don't know what to do," he told his daughter.

"Oh no, Dad. It seemed so perfect," she said.

Then an idea came to him. "I just had a thought. You were talking about getting a job at the boys' school. Maybe you could come up here to take care of your mom instead. I'll pay you. She'll be fine with you in the house."

"That's a great idea. I'll start on Monday!"

It seemed to be a perfect plan. Mel would drop the boys off at school then head north to her parent's house. She would keep an eye on her mom, prepare meals for them both, pack her dad's lunches for the week, tend to laundry, and clean the house. She would then leave to be at the boys' school in time to pick them up and take care of her own family. This only left Gaye alone for a short time until Eric would arrive from work. It was a great win-win situation for everyone—at first.

But as days turned into weeks, it was becoming more and more difficult for Mel to be at the house with her mother. Gaye seemed to distrust her daughter, telling her that she thought she was stealing from her. When Mel pleaded innocence to her mom, Gaye snapped at her and told her not to call her Mom, that she was not her daughter. Her daughter would not be stealing from her! It was heart wrenching for Mel. Her mother not only didn't recognize her anymore, but Gaye despised this stranger, yelling and cursing at her to leave her home.

Mel called her father. "I can't help Mom anymore. She hates me, she absolutely hates me. I think it's time she went into a facility," she pleaded with him.

"No, I think I can still take care of her for a while, Mel. You have done so much; thank you for trying," he told her.

Day after day, Gaye became more distant, quiet, and incapable of being alone. She accused Eric of doing things behind her back. "What are you doing to me?" she'd shout.

The words cut like a knife into the very soul of Eric. "I'm not doing anything, Gaye, really," he'd try to convince her.

Then it happened. Eric came home from work to check on Gaye. She ordered him out of the house, yelling and screaming at him. She seemed to not know him or not trust him—or both. All he knew is that she wouldn't let him in the house. Eric, desperate and not knowing what else to do, called Dr. Mayfield. After being instructed to call the paramedics, Eric called 911. When the paramedics put Gaye into the ambulance, Eric felt as though he had betrayed his wife; it was a difficult decision, but it had to be done. Eric called Mel to meet him at the hospital.

After examining Gaye at the hospital, Dr. Mayfield said, "It's time she went into an Alzheimer's unit. There's no way to care for her at home anymore." The words were painful to hear but also came as a relief to both Eric and Mel. Mel called Rix right away. "We've got to find a place for Mom. I'm going to stay here until I find one," she told him.

"Emily and I will be there as soon as we can to help," Rix replied.

It was an agonizing quest. Where would they put the mother who had so lovingly raised them? Where would this young woman, sentenced with this terrifying disease, live out the rest of her shortened life? Where would she live in a confusing world of silence and loneliness, without memories or loved ones around her? Where?

After days of searching, the family found an Alzheimer's unit; it wasn't perfect but no place would be. Rix, Emily, Brian, Megan, Mel, Madlyn and Eric were with Gaye when she was taken to the unit. Mel kept a low profile due to fear of making Gaye angry when she saw her, remembering the hatred on her mother's face the last day she'd spent with her at their home. Mel slipped into Gaye's room and set it up with furnishings and art from her parents' home, to make it feel more familiar for her.

Mel then planned to leave, so as not to upset Gaye. She told her father and he replied, "Mel, it will be fine. You need to be here with your mom," he said, feeling that he needed her support. Mel stayed; she understood that he needed her.

When they all first approached the home, Gaye refused to go into the building. She seemed to know that it was a place she didn't want to be in. Madlyn took Rix aside and explained to him that she thought Gaye would listen to her son. Rix "stepped up to the plate" and talked his mother into going in.

He would later confide to me that he felt as though he had betrayed his mother that day. When he told me this, I explained to him that his mother needed the care she would get from this home, and that he was such a loving son to convince her that it was a place she wanted to be.

To Mel's relief, when Gaye finally walked into the home and saw her daughter, she greeted her with a welcoming hello. Gaye repeatedly asked her children, whether they thought her home was beautiful; she seemed happy and content with her surroundings. After their visit, everyone departed, leaving Eric alone with his wife. They had dinner together and visited in Gaye's new room. As Eric began to ready himself to leave, fear came over Gaye's face and she pleaded, "Don't leave me here, please don't leave me here. I don't like this place; take me home, please, Eric, take me home."

The words were painful for Eric to hear as he realized that she knew it was not her home. She understood enough that it was frightening to her. Eric spent night after night with Gaye in her room, trying to comfort her and ease her into her "new home." When he attempted to leave, the pain and anguish he felt forced him to stay yet another night with her. Finally, by day five, the transition was made, and Eric went home to his empty house.

As he opened the door to the house he would have collapsed if it hadn't been for his two faithful dogs, Parker and Bit. They were excited to see him and helped Eric push the pain away for a few more moments. He tended to the dogs and sat in his chair. He looked around his house, the pain and tears welling up in his heart and eyes. He felt defeated; Alzheimer's had won. He no longer had his wife and was left only with a shattering diagnosis—and this house. The house that Gaye had fallen in love with and wanted so desperately. The house in which they were to, perhaps, have grown old in. The house of Gaye's last real Christmas. The house of lost dreams, painful memories and bleeding hearts.

CHAPTER 5

MOVING ON

I don't pretend to be a devout Christian, by most definitions. In the past, my excuse for not regularly attending church, although poor, was that my husband was agnostic and wouldn't participate in anything spiritual. I also used the excuse that churches were hypocritical. I raised my children, when little, in a Lutheran Church. Tim initially attended with us, but after a while he left and announced that he was agnostic. It was difficult to keep teenage children in church, and to attend myself, when their father wasn't supporting the idea.

But I know my relationship with God. I like to call myself spiritual. When I am faced with life challenges, my daily prayers and talks with God increase. He is my strength and the one that got me through my childhood with such a positive attitude. I know he placed me in my home for a reason; I accept it and love Him all the more for it. Once in the mountains, deep in prayer, I felt God's love and knew what I needed to do.

It was late in February of 2005, when I took my solitary trip to the mountains. When I arrived home from my brief retreat, I could see in Tim's eyes that he knew. He and I were comfortable with each other and talked about every aspect of our parting. Although there was pain, we knew we would be all right. Telling the children, however, would be difficult.

Mark, who had guessed at age thirteen that Tim and I didn't belong together, seemed to accept the idea at once. Brad tried to make it appear as though it didn't faze him, but I knew better. He was away at school, so he could hide from the pain and reality. But his pain manifested in a way that could have killed him. He became heavily involved with drugs during this time. He was immature and perhaps not ready to go to college, even though his age said he was. He now says that it was the immaturity that caused his bout with drugs; I take comfort in that idea but feel the impending divorce didn't help. Amanda was deeply saddened. She was young and it hurt. Tim and I reassured her as best we could, but only time and healing would ease her pain.

Our other problem was: Now, how to tell the parents? We made a "date" with my dad and stepmother for dinner. My parents had finally divorced when I was seventeen. My dad remarried a beautiful woman that my children know as Mamaw. She is a grandmother to them in every sense of the word. There is no "step" in our love for her. At dinner with them, at one of our family's favorite pizza places, the kids went to the playroom and I told them.

"Tim and I are getting divorced," I signed to them. They seemed to not understand what I said. I signed again, "Tim and I have decided that we love each other, but we are not happy and are going to divorce." They looked stunned.

"Oh, you and Tim are going to divorce?" my dad signed as if only going through the motions to understand the thoughts presented to him.

"Yes, we are going to divorce. I will be moving into an apartment in March," I signed to them both.

"You are not happy?" my stepmom signed to us both.

"No, we haven't been happy for a long time," Tim signed to her.

"Oh well, we support you both and hope you will be happy," my dad signed back.

I could tell they still didn't get it. To everyone, including our parents, Tim and I had the perfect marriage. We were always so happy and affectionate with each other. We did love each other, but the relationship wasn't satisfying either one of us emotionally or spiritually—we both needed to find what it was that we needed.

My parents were the easy ones to tell. But telling my father-in-law, Melvin? That was going to hurt, as my love and respect for him was immense. His love and respect for me meant the world to me. He was a father to me, but how could I tell him? I didn't want to risk the relationship I had with him. I was afraid he would shun me and, thinking he needed to take a side, support Tim and push me away. I couldn't lose him, but I couldn't stay married to his son just for the sake of my relationship with him. Yet I was very afraid to tell him.

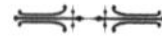

Trying to keep the declining family business going, we had begun to move the shop into Tim's basement during the time I was to move out. Business was really bad, as the economy was affecting us like everyone else. Melvin sold the business property and moved into the house that Granny had once lived in. He moved the engraving portion of the business into one of the bedrooms. He'd lost his wife five years previously and still missed her dearly; her picture graced every nook and cranny of his living room. This was the kind of love and devotion that I wanted from my partner, I remember thinking.

One day, while organizing files in the basement, I said to Tim, "I don't know how to tell your dad. I'm so afraid of what he'll think of me."

Putting the box down that he was carrying, he put his hand on my shoulder and said, "You know my dad loves you. He won't think anything bad of you. We both want this; this is not a messy divorce.

We are just parting as a married couple. We are still friends and still parents to our kids. His feelings won't change at all. You'll see." With tears in my eyes, I nodded my head in agreement, but my heart was still afraid.

"Look, I'm on my way over there now. I can tell him if you'd like. That way I can get a feel for how he's going to handle this," he said, trying to comfort me.

My stomach was in knots waiting for Tim to return. My cell phone rang; it was Tim: "Hey, Tami." It was odd to hear him call me Tami when for more than twenty five years I had been "honey.") I've talked to my dad and Uncle Dee (Melvin's younger brother) too. They are both here and want you to come over." They were at the shop cleaning up the remnants from the last thirty-two years.

I drove up and, gathering my strength, I walked in the shop door. The years Melvin and I had spent running the business—me helping to take care of the shop, Granny and even him—made for a close bond between us. As I entered the shop, I noticed how empty it all looked and felt. Except for a few chairs and a filing cabinet, there wasn't anything that spoke of the thriving business it once had been. The emptiness of the shop made me ache even more than I already did at the thought of facing my "dad."

Melvin was sitting and Uncle Dee was standing. The moment I saw Melvin, I burst into tears. He got up and wrapped his arms around me and gave me a reassuring hug.

As he pulled away from our embrace, he signed, "You will always be my daughter. I have always called you my daughter; nothing will change. I want both you and Tim to be happy. I told Dee, not too long ago," he continued as we both sat down, "that I wouldn't be surprised if you and Tim divorced sometime, because you are two very different people; I don't understand how you both were happy. Didn't I?" he signed as he pointed to his brother. It was then that I realized how deep my bond with Melvin was; he knew me so well. He saw what others couldn't.

"Yes," Uncle Dee signed back, and then he added, "you will always be my niece; you are always part of the family."

"I still will need to depend on you, as always, if that is OK?" Melvin asked me.

"Of course, you know I will always take care of you and the business. I need you in my life," I signed back.

Relief set in—I still had my "dad" and I would be allowed to continue to take care of him. With the hardest part of my divorce over and my needs fulfilled, I was excited about getting on with my new life!

Tim was, and will always be, family to me but I was ready to find my life partner, the love of my life. I knew he existed, I knew he was out there. I wanted to find him, my knight in shining armor, and I knew I *would* find him.

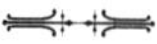

A few days later I was sitting in my new apartment, by myself; I wondered about my life ahead of me. The dream I had the night before seemed to be a look into my future. Just then my phone rang.

"Hey Tami, how are you?" I heard a familiar southern drawl.

"Hi Wynne, I'm good, how are you?" I asked. Wynne is a childhood friend—we'd met at the age of nine when we went to Girl Scout camp. We have been friends ever since; she is the kind of friend you consider family. We've seen each other through a lot: our marriages, the birth of her son, my children, her divorce and now mine. We can go months without connecting, but the moment we hear each other's voices, it's as if we picked up from where we left off the day before.

"I've been thinking about you a lot lately. Been worried and hoping you're OK. A divorce, good or bad, is always difficult," she said.

"I'm good, really I am. Tim and I are talking a lot; we both know this is what we both want. Really, if there is such a thing, we are having a great divorce," I told her. "But I had an odd dream last night,"

I continued. "I was in a strange house, someplace I don't recognize. It was morning and I came from the bedroom. I walked around a staircase and saw a handsome man with dark hair standing in the kitchen, drinking something. He had on a white dress shirt with a tie. It looked like he was getting ready to go to work. The kitchen was nice and big and looked like one I'd love to cook in. Anyway, he looked at me with so much love in his eyes, I felt so blessed!"

"Maybe he's your man. Maybe you'll meet this man someday," she said.

"I sure hope so," I told her. "At least I hope I get that feeling from someone someday. That feeling of complete love for me. Anyway, his tie was crooked, so I needed to straighten it for him; it was like he needed me but, at the same time, the love I felt from him was so deep and pure, it was amazing."

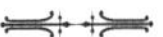

I began dating and dated a lot. Having lost almost 150 pounds, I looked and felt great! I had not dated in high school (except Tim) and really wanted to enjoy the experience. I knew that although I was having a good time dating, I really wanted to be married in a couple of years. I loved marriage; I loved the thought of sharing my life with someone and being truly in love with him, and him with me. But I wasn't going to settle; I wanted to find my true "knight in shining armor"—the soul mate that came to me in a dream. After that dream, I knew he was out there. Because of my spirituality and relationship with God, I knew the dream was sent to reassure me that he was out there, that God had someone planned for me. I just needed to be patient that my "knight" was waiting for me as well.

I worked, dated and dealt with family issues. The divorce was hard on Amanda. She was angry at me for moving out of the house. I tried to include her in decisions for dishes and furnishings for "our" new apartment, so she would be excited. She just wanted to be home. I understood. It was the only home she knew. Her dogs and cat were there, even though I wasn't, so she wanted to be there.

Brad had quit college after his first semester, due to the drugs. He said he had to get away from the drugs before they killed him. He moved back into his father's house. As I mentioned earlier, he is one of the smartest people I have ever known, but his lack of common sense can get the best of him sometimes. He found a good job and is manager of the store he works for. He has recently decided that he needs to go back to school; those are the words I have been praying to hear for a very long time.

Mark has always battled depression. In the past, he was able to pull himself from it. When he was a small child, I saw that he was an actor. He was so involved with his "play" that one would think he truly believed he was Peter Pan, Captain America, Robin (of Batman and Robin) or any character he was playing. But society dictated differently. There is no room for "acting" in our society. The chances of making money at "make believe" are slim to none. So Mark conformed. He went to school, as society dictated, and battled depression. He seemed to cope well with the divorce. Or so I thought at the time.

One day, my younger sister called to tell me that our Uncle Milt had just died. Milt was my dad's brother and my mom's partner for the past four years—long story. "Mike and I are going out to California to move Mom here," my sister informed me. My mom had been battling lymphoma for a year, and although the cancer was in remission, Naomi felt that she needed to take care of her.

"I'll get a plane ticket and see you out there," I told her.

My mom and I weren't close. We went through typical mother-daughter fights, and for a brief time afterward, grew close. But circumstances changed, and while I love my mother very much, I don't have a lot of respect for her. Strange, she once told me much the same about her relationship with her mother.

It was about this time that I had an appointment with a psychologist for Amanda. I felt that she needed someone to talk to about the divorce.

One day, I was talking on the phone to Mark, who had just started his senior year in high school. "Mom," he said, "I can't get myself out of the depression this time. It's eating me up. I don't know what's wrong".

I told him I had the appointment for Amanda, but maybe she would see Mark instead. He agreed.

We went to the office and when I explained to the psychologist the need for Mark to be seen, she was willing. After about ten minutes, she came out of the room and said, "I am worried. Mark has agreed to check himself into Cedar Springs (a local psychiatric hospital). He doesn't have a plan, but he is suicidal."

I had a feeling. From the way Mark had been talking, I knew the depression was bad this time.

Mark checked himself in on Wednesday. On Friday, the day I was to leave for California, I met with the care team at the facility. The psychiatrist stated, "Mark is not suicidal. He is a person who gives of himself to the brink of his own destruction. He needs to move from his father's house. He is taking care of his father, sister, brother, and friends—everyone but himself. That's why he can't get out of this depression."

"I'd like to talk to him please," I said.

I met Mark in the common room. He said, in desperation, "Mom, get me out of here. These people are going to make me crazy. I don't belong here. Please!"

I spoke again to the doctor. "He's not suicidal; I can't hold him here," he explained. "But you have to promise me to move him out of his father's house."

"Absolutely," I said. "I am going to California today but will move him as soon as I get back."

"You don't understand. No, he either goes to California with you or you don't go," he insisted. That's all it took. I understood. I got a plane ticket for Mark and we headed to California.

On our return, Mark and I moved to a larger apartment. He drifted back and forth between his father's place and mine. He got involved with drugs, quit school and was spiraling out of control.

One day, when I was at his father's house tending to the family business, Mark complained incessantly about not being able to figure out what he was supposed to be doing. It was then that I finally got angry and said, "You need to get yourself together and work things out, one step at a time. Get your GED, find out what colleges accept a GED and get on with your life. You're the one who has always said that you need to get living your 'real' life. So do it!"

I was angry but scared. I couldn't bear to lose my relationship with him but I knew he was going to spiral downward. It wasn't long after I left that he did just that. But he pulled himself together enough to scour the Internet for a university that accepted a GED. He found a performing arts university in San Francisco and applied. He could go back to who he was born to be, an actor! My guilt and pain over his depression will never be erased, but my heart fills with hope and love knowing that Mark is doing what he is supposed to be doing; he is no longer conforming to what society dictates and is following his dream.

The guilt of the divorce was unbearable at times. I will never say I handled it the "right way" as far as my kids are concerned. But I did the best I could with the skills I had. I put faith in my "inner voice" and set my sights on our future. I relied heavily on prayer and my friends for support. I felt that I was doing the right thing...Or was I? Tim, of all people, assured me that we were doing the best thing and that we would all be OK. I hoped he was right. I prayed, hoped, loved my kids and waited. Only time would tell.

CHAPTER 6

MENDING A BROKEN HEART

When I met him at Starbucks on October 13, 2007, it was with no expectations. But in the days to follow, I soon discovered that my life would never be the same.

We met online through a dating service. I had joined the dating service six months before I met him. I quit after a month of being on the service, because most of the people I was meeting didn't match the profiles that they had on the site. Once you quit the service, though, they keep your picture and profile available so people can still send you "winks," which are "I'm interested" signals. I ignored them all until September of that year when I received a "wink" from a man named Eric.

Since I was no longer a member, I had to pay the membership fee so that I could email him to let him know I was interested. I don't know what it was about his profile or what it said. I didn't even care for his picture, but I was interested in this man who was picking grapes in one of his profile pictures. I sent him an email and promptly explained that he should feel special because I had to pay to email him.

He emailed back, and as we conversed over a few emails, my interest in him grew.

It was about this time that my son Mark and I went to California for my grandmother's funeral. After we returned, Eric emailed me asking to finally meet at a Starbucks. I was excited at meeting this man who had piqued my interest.

I had no expectations about this meeting. I knew this man interested me for some reason and I wanted to find out why. At the very least, I thought it would be a nice way to spend a Saturday afternoon. Arriving at the coffee shop, I spotted him sitting at an outside table. As I studied him there, I thought that his eyes looked soulful when they met mine and that he seemed unsure about our encounter. He was a handsome man, and his smile lit up his eyes when he realized who I was. We made our introductions, ordered our drinks and sat outside to chat. We talked about our children, our lives and what our hopes were as a result of being on the dating service.

He then went on and told me he had type 1 diabetes and had undergone a double bypass operation the year before. I remember thinking, "This man needs taking care of." I needed to proceed cautiously or perhaps I'd jump into something for the wrong reasons again. It was a skill taught to me in therapy, to recognize feelings for what they were and not to make them into something they weren't. It seemed as though Eric were giving me his health history as a way to determine if I was still interested.

"I'm a nurse. I know what diabetes is and I know what a bypass is. You seem to be pretty healthy by the look of you; I'm sure you're taking care of yourself quite well," I told him.

"Yes, my cardiologist said my heart is in great condition. I have no neuropathy or any serious side effects from my diabetes," he assured me.

We chitchatted a while longer; then I asked him about his married life. In an email, prior to our meeting, he told me that he had to explain it to me in person, that there was too much to explain in an email. I worried that he was still married and perhaps cheating on his wife when he emailed me that, but I was open minded, perhaps naïve, and met him anyway. What he did tell me, I was not prepared for.

"So, Eric, you didn't want to discuss your marital situation in emails," I finally got the courage to say him. "So what is it? Are you married?" I asked.

"It's a long, painful story, but one that I need to tell you. My wife of twenty-nine years is in a nursing home. She was diagnosed with probable early-onset Alzheimer's disease. After a quick progression of the disease brought us back to the United States when we were living in Europe, she was diagnosed in 2003," he said. The tears in his eyes gave me a glimpse of the pain he must have endured.

The nurse in me felt a sudden attraction to this man with all his pain. I reached over to touch his arm as he continued, "She rapidly deteriorated to the point where I couldn't care for her anymore at home. She no longer knows anyone; I don't even think she recognizes me anymore. She has been under hospice care for six months now." A tear rolled down his cheek and his lips quivered as he tried to recompose himself.

My heart ached for him, and my own eyes filled with tears for his pain. How dare a disease for the elderly take his wife from him and their children at such a young age! I had never heard of "early-onset" Alzheimer's and wanted to know more, but I was afraid to cause him any more pain in this public venue. I continued to stroke his arm to try and ease the pain he was feeling. I didn't really know how a stranger stroking his arm could bring much comfort, but I'm a nurse—it's what I do.

"I'm so sorry, Eric," I finally said, wiping away my own tears. "How is your family dealing with all this?" I asked him.

"They are all handling it well. It's been a difficult few years. Gaye, my wife, is in a great place that takes really good care of her. I visit her every day and bring her juice. On the weekends, I bring the staff donuts and give her one as well," he explained, looking at me as if he thought I was going to run away at what he was telling me. I looked into his green eyes and now understood why they were so soulful. Eric had endured so much in the past few years—and this explained why he appeared the way he did to me. I continued to look into his eyes with care and understanding of his pain and felt a connection with this stranger who had just opened his heart to me.

"That's wonderful that she's in such a great facility. Where is it?" I asked.

"Life Care Center, on International Circle," he told me.

"I live in the apartments just to the north of there," I said in surprise at the irony of it.

"Wow! Isn't that strange!" Eric said. "I've been in your proximity quite a bit and never knew it." He then shook his head, as if to clear his mind of the subject and said, "Let's talk about something else. Look, I am going to a Halloween party in two weeks at Barracuda Bob's; it's a local pub near where I live. I'd love to take you, if you'd like to go."

I accepted at once, probably sounding more than a bit overexcited. "I love Halloween, and I *love* that you want to go and, more importantly, that you want me to go with you!" I told him.

"It's a pirate's ball. Do you know of a costume shop where we could rent pirate outfits?" he asked me.

"Yes, there's one on Fillmore, or it's off Fillmore. I have some time right now if you want to go look real quick," I offered.

"Sure, I'll follow you, since you know where you're going" he said as he got up and motioned to pull my chair out for me. "Give me your number, in case I get lost," he said as we stood. I hadn't given him my number before our meeting, because I'd had a few not-so-great experiences in the past. We exchanged our cell phone numbers and he walked me to my car. I promptly called information to get the address and drove up to the parking lot exit, waiting for him to pull up behind me. After a fifteen minute drive, we found the costume shop. We had such a good time trying on different costumes; we laughed and joked at the different outfits as we tried them on. I already felt at ease with this man whom I had only just met; it was comfortable. Once we'd decided on the costumes, we reserved them and walked toward our cars.

"What are your plans for the rest of the day?" he asked.

"I have a family function to go to, then Mark, my son, is having a party at my apartment, so I'm having dinner with a girlfriend and staying the night at her place," I explained.

"What are your plans?" I asked him.

"No plans, I'll be home. Call me later?" he asked.

"Of course I will. I had a great time trying on costumes with you. I can't wait for the pirate's ball—it sounds like fun."

"It will be," he said. We hugged each other good-bye, and I drove toward my ex-sister-in-law's house for Uncle Dee's birthday party.

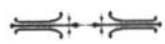

As I drove, I couldn't stop thinking about the man I had just met. His love and devotion to his wife were so admirable. Secretly, I felt envious—I wanted someone to love me that way. I wanted to know this man more; I wanted to spend more time with him; I wanted to reconnect with him, even after only being away from him for such a brief time. Going against my better judgment, I followed my heart and called him while driving to the party.

"Hi, it's me, Tami," I said when he answered in his now-familiar deep voice. "I was listening to the radio and wondered what kind of music you like."

"All kinds," he said as he named off a few of his favorite bands. I recognized only a few of the names he rattled off. "And you?" he asked.

"I like all kinds too, except for heavy metal. But country music is my favorite. You probably hate country music, don't you?" I asked playfully.

"No, like I said, I like all kinds. Besides, I don't think it matters if we don't like the exact same music. We can learn about each other's music and maybe learn to like a new genre," he said.

I agreed and we made small talk for the rest of my drive. As I neared my destination, we said our good-byes and he asked me to call him as soon as I could. I promised that I would. It was strange that I felt so attracted to this beautiful man who had such devotion to his life partner. The jealousy I felt was not because of his wife but came from my longing for comparable emotion to be directed toward me. I wondered if Eric's capacity for devotion was, perhaps, part of my attraction to him.

As I sat in my car in front of my ex-sister-in-law's house, gathering my things, my thoughts began to drift to the conversation about Eric's wife. My heart ached for him and Gaye. His wife of twenty-nine-plus years was sentenced to live out her final years without the memories she had made and filed away in the recesses of her mind. I felt the hot tears filling my eyes again; I had to compose myself or everyone at the party would be asking what the matter was.

I looked in the mirror to check my makeup. Looking at my own green eyes, I thought of Eric's. There was something about those eyes that drew me in. I wanted to spend more time with this gentle soul. We hadn't made another date, except for the Halloween party in two weeks. Perhaps I could call him tomorrow to set up another meeting, I thought to myself. He did ask me to call him as soon as I could, so maybe I should call him sooner? Oh brother! For now, I needed to stop thinking about him and get in to the party.

The party was joyful and fun. It was Tim's family, but mine as well. They would always be my family, and I enjoyed being with them. No uneasiness, just family—it was such a great day!

After the family gathering, I headed back to my apartment with Mark. I changed my clothes to meet my friend for dinner and issued instructions for Mark: "You and your friends need to behave tonight.

Don't be too loud and disturb the neighbors. I'm trusting you to behave," I told him in my best "Mamma voice.'"

"I know, Mamma, it'll be fine, I promise," he said as he scooted me out the door.

As I drove to meet my girlfriend, thoughts of Eric were heavy on my mind. I felt such a strong urge to call him that I didn't resist it for long.

"Come out here," he said, once we'd said our hellos. "I'd love the company and want to get to know you some more."

I agreed and promised to call him for directions once I had finished dinner. Even though I had just met him, I trusted him. I knew I was breaking a dating rule by going to his house, but nothing about meeting him or hearing his story fit with any rules that I knew.

After getting instructions from Eric, I drove out to a grocery store near his home; he met me there, and I followed him to his house. At the door, a cute little "pig"-looking dog greeted me. "This is Bit; she's a miniature bull terrier," he said as he introduced us.

"Nice to meet you, Bit," I said as I kneeled down beside her. We made friends quickly. I could tell right away that she had a very sweet disposition, like her owner.

Eric escorted me through the laundry room and into a large kitchen that opened up into a living room. He showed me to a rocking chair and took a seat in an adjacent chair. We talked for hours, just as though we were old friends catching up. I felt so comfortable with this handsome man, as if I had known him from before. We talked of our lives up to that point, our jobs, our hopes and dreams. I kept my promise to my girlfriend and texted her often to let her know I was safe. After several assurances that I was fine, I told her that I wasn't going to text anymore. Eric then introduced me to German schnapps and took me on a tour of the house. It was a beautiful house. But I noticed that there weren't any pictures anywhere and it was missing a woman's touch. I assumed Gaye became too ill to really make the house hers.

It was getting late and I had drunk a little too many schnapps to drive home safely. Eric suggested I stay the night. I'm sure the look on my face prompted him to quickly say, "I'm not suggesting anything, really. I'll lend you some pajamas and you can sleep in the guestroom if you like." He was truly being a gentleman and just like earlier that day, I knew I could trust him.

"OK, I'd like that. I shouldn't drive right now anyway," I told him smiling. As I changed my clothes in the bathroom I felt a warm feeling inside as if I were where I belonged. Not necessarily in the house, but with Eric. I quickly chalked it up to the schnapps!

I came out of the bathroom and met Eric who was standing there smiling. His smile warmed my heart. "This man is having some kind of powerful effect on me…How can this be?" I wondered to myself.

We talked a bit more and Eric said, "I'd like to share my bed with you. I promise, nothing more than holding you, if you'll let me."

How could I say no? Whether it was the schnapps or not, I didn't want to be without him for one moment either.

We climbed into his bed. What should have been awkward and uncomfortable wasn't. I moved closer to him. He wrapped his strong arms around me and said good night. I couldn't get over how comfortable I felt. It seemed to me that I was meant to be here, in his arms, like we were two puzzle pieces finally put back together after being separated in the box since we were first cut out. "Eric?" I asked in a shy voice. "I don't usually kiss on the first date..."

"Yes, you told me that," he said.

"But, technically, our first date was at Starbucks today," I said, "so this is our second date, right?"

He knew what I was leading to. I lifted my lips to his and was suddenly lost in a passionate kiss that I'll never forget. Strangely enough, it was a kiss that felt familiar. Realizing that I was putting myself in a compromising position, I made the motions to end our kiss. I knew it wouldn't be long before I would make love to him. I sunk back into his arms and we drifted off to sleep.

The next morning I made Eric breakfast and headed home. I hated leaving him; the fear that I would lose what I had just found frightened me. I felt as though I were crazy! I spent the next day talking to him on the phone several times and trying to figure things out.

"I'd like to see you again tomorrow," he said.

We agreed to meet the next evening at eight, after I'd finished work. I could hardly wait. My head was spinning and I felt the warm feeling again, but this time I knew it wasn't the schnapps!

CHAPTER 7

LOVE MOVING QUICKLY

We met that night at Champs. Seeing him again, my heart swelled with the warm feelings that I told myself were sexual attraction. Nonetheless, I was so glad to get an eyeful of him again. But more importantly, I got to be near him and hold his hand. As we talked, we were, once again, the only people who existed.

I was exhausted from my busy twelve-hour schedule but had newfound energy sitting next to him with his arm around me. I had recently transferred from the pediatric floor to the emergency room and was telling Eric of my day. "They are talking about trauma training me already. I am worried it will be too tough for me. But I feel obligated to do the training, because they were so great about moving me into the ER to begin with," I explained.

"Why do you think it will be so tough?" he asked. "Do you think it will be too gruesome for you?"

"No, the testing is supposed to be tough. I have heard of people having to take it more than once. I get test anxiety really bad, so I am afraid I'll never pass it."

"Don't worry. If they didn't think you were capable, I'm sure they wouldn't go to the trouble," he said in a confident voice.

There it was—the kind of reassurance I thought I should have with the man I was with. It was this genuine confidence in me, albeit from a virtual stranger, that I desired from my life partner. We continued our conversation and listened to each other's day. Then, once again, we had to say good-bye. We kissed goodnight and parted to go to our respective homes.

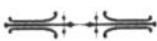

For the longest time, really ever since I can remember, I had always felt as though a part of me was missing. But when I was with Eric, I felt whole. It seemed crazy, because I had just met him; I couldn't explain it—I just knew what I felt. I analyzed it up and down, inside and out, but still came up with the same feelings. The next few weeks, I challenged my every move, my every thought, my every feeling. I would not enter into another relationship on the premise of "warm feelings." I wanted to know why I had the "warm feelings" and it needed to be for the right reasons.

Ever since the night we met at Champs, we texted constantly. We talked on the phone whenever we could. We were pretty much inseparable when not at work. Then, one day while at his house, he told me, "My daughter Melanie wants to meet you. We'll meet them at Old Chicago's for dinner."

Realizing that he must have spoken to her about me, I felt as though he must feel something similar to what I was feeling. I was elated but also anxious.

"Really? You and I just met, ourselves," I said, somewhat trying to get out of it.

"Yes, but she has heard so much about you from me, and really wants to meet you. They'll come up from Pueblo on Thursday night. You can meet me here and we'll go together," he said.

"Them?" I asked.

"Yes, her husband Jamie and their three boys. Nathan is the oldest, and Chris and Josh are the twins," he explained. Of course, not wanting to disappoint him, I agreed.

We arrived at the restaurant and found the table where Mel and her family were sitting. As we walked up to the table, they all stood up to greet us. We said our hellos and then began the real conversation. I was quite nervous, but not about Mel and her family liking me. My nervousness stemmed from the situation. I knew that, some time ago, Eric's children, family, and even Gaye's own mother had encouraged Eric to move on and find someone so that he could be happy. But since the situation was so unusual, I didn't know what to think at this meeting. But I soon found that the conversation was easy and that I liked Mel right away.

Jamie was quiet but seemed to be perceptively studying the conversation. The boys joined in when they could. Being one who loves children, I drew them into conversation, which proved easy. I loved them all; they seemed to be like family and, best of all, made me feel like family. We spoke in an easy way, as though we were catching up since the last time we had seen each other. After dinner we all walked to their car. Mel reached out her arms to hug me. Whew—she liked me!

A few months later, Mel told me that she was determined not to like me on that first meeting. To help with that resolve, she had even worn her mom's favorite perfume and her mom's coat. Then she said, "But it was not long after we started talking that I realized you were nice and that I already liked you. There was no 'not liking you,' no matter what mind-set I had. You fit in with the family as if you were always there. But more importantly, my dad was smiling. That was all I needed—I hadn't seen him smile like that in years!" It was wonderful to know that she felt that way, because, believe it or not, I not only liked her and her family. I had a love for them already.

I have often thought of Melanie's response to meeting me that first time. Perhaps it was a way to protect her mom and to keep the "wrong" woman out of her dad's life. Or maybe it was because her mom was still living that she felt the need to be so determined not to like the woman her dad was introducing her to. Regardless, Mel acted the way she needed to, considering the circumstances. After all, how does a daughter accept another woman in her father's life when her mother is still living, and the couple still married? Mel conducted herself with respect and grace; she did it in a way that made me proud of her, and I know her mother would have been too.

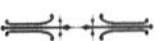

The next morning, Eric got a call from Mel. "Dad, I really liked her! She seems so sweet. The boys loved her! But don't you think she dresses really young?"

"Well, Mel, she had a gastric bypass a few years ago and—" Eric started.

"Oh! That's why. I get it, Dad. She looks fabulous! Boy, she's quite the 'trophy wife,' don't you think?"

"I've just met her and you're already calling her my wife?" he asked.

"Well, you never know..." she said. "Where is she now? Are you going to see her today?"

"She's in the kitchen making my breakfast," he told her matter-of-factly. "Dad!" she exclaimed with pretended shock. They both chuckled and, after talking a bit more, hung up. Eric then busied himself in the bedroom while waiting for his breakfast. After breakfast, he took me into the bedroom and led me to Gaye's closet. He had cleared away her clothes and had them in a pile in a trunk that was in the room. "I'd like you to move some of your things here, so it's more convenient for you when you're staying," he told me. His eyes looked pleased as he showed me the closet.

"I agreed and we hugged, both excited at everything that was new in our relationship.

Eric moved to the trunk to close it. His hesitancy made me realize what he was doing—and what he was having to face.

I moved closer to give him comfort. "Eric, this must be hard. I can't imagine what must be going through your mind right now. Please, share with me," I said as I motioned for him to sit on the bed next to me.

"It has to be done. It should have been done a long time ago. I'm glad I'm doing it now, especially because it's for you," he explained.

"Tell me about Gaye. I'd like to know her," I said. From the start, I had wanted to know more about the woman he loved so deeply—the mother of his children and the one he was supposed to grow old with. I wanted to know her so that I, too, might love her.

"Tell me how you met," I suggested.

As the story unfolded, I realized he hadn't visited his memories in a long time. I was full of questions, about Gaye, their life together, and the children. I wanted to know all of it; I wanted to know the woman that had won his heart, all those years ago. As he spoke of their lives, his lip began to quiver and his eyes teared up.

"What's making you so sad?" I asked.

"I don't know—it's all so sad."

"I know the situation is sad, but the memories that you're sharing with me are good, happy memories. Shouldn't they make you feel somewhat happy?"

"Yes, you're right. But I can't help but feel sad for her. It's just such a heartbreaking situation. She didn't deserve this," he added.

"Neither did you," I told him as the tears rose in my eyes.

The day was long and exhausting, but Eric shared every detail from his memory that he could. I felt a connection to him so deep that it dizzied me. And because Eric was able to paint such an accurate picture of his wife, I also felt a connection to Gaye. That night, lying in his arms while he drifted off to sleep, I began analyzing my feelings. I knew that my connection to him was not only that of a woman with feelings for a man, but also that of a nurse consoling a patient. I also recognized that I am a person who needs this in my everyday life—not just at work, but in my personal life as well. I had strong feelings for this man who needed me but understood that I needed him as well. Feeling at peace with the "work" that had been done, knowing my former therapist would be proud, I welcomed sleep after such an emotionally draining day.

I relished the warmth and smell of Eric as I snuggled closer to him. His strong arms embraced me tighter. Drifting off to sleep, I realized I was exactly where I was supposed to be, exactly where I wanted to be, and I was falling in love for the first time in my life.

Our incessant texting, even at work, was going to get me into trouble and was costing Eric a fortune. When we weren't texting, we were talking to each other on the phone. I stopped going home to my apartment and started staying at Eric's house more and more. The night of the pirate's ball came quickly. I picked up the costumes and headed to his house. We had so much fun dressing up for the party. We looked great, especially Eric, who resembled Captain Jack Sparrow, only a lot taller!

I was to meet his friends at this party, so I was a bit nervous. They knew his story, and I felt some anxiety about what they would think of me. My fears were for naught; his friends embraced me for what I was, Eric's girlfriend. The female friends he had made seemed to be a little cold to me—understandably so, as Eric is very handsome and perhaps they all had a crush on him, even the married ones. Once we were having fun, I didn't care what anyone thought. I was with Eric, which was all that I'd wanted from the day I'd met him. I was secure in the knowledge that Eric needed me, and that I needed him more than I needed to breathe.

As far as my family life went at this time, I am ashamed to say that I "checked out" as Mom. I am not proud of this and regret that things went the way they did, but I can't change that now. My sons took over my apartment and, in one way, it was the best thing that could have happened to them both. They became friends again. These were brothers who, as children, had played side-by-side every day, pretending to be Batman and Robin, fighting the bad guys together. But adolescence drove a wedge between these once-close, but very different, brothers. Something changed when they were living together in the apartment, and it brought them together again. It comforts me to know that, in the time I was away from them, they were able to find each other again.

It was different with Amanda. She was still young. I had set up a room for her at Eric's house for when she would stay with us. She loved "her room"; I painted it a beautiful lavender color with striking accent colors on the bed and in the wall art. I know, in the beginning, her heart wasn't really there when she stayed with us. This was new territory for us all; we would just take it one day at a time.

I was busy investing all of my time and effort in this man who needed me and whom I needed. But I began to ache for my sons to know Eric—this man whom I knew I was destined to be with. Amanda had already begun a relationship with him and, I was sure, given her brothers a glimpse of him from her perspective. I figured that what she had to say wouldn't be very flattering for, of course, Amanda wasn't going to like anyone I met, because he wasn't her father. I just asked them all to get to know him and to be open to who he was. Sitting on the couch in the apartment one afternoon, I was talking to Mark about Eric.

"Mom, I'm so happy for you," my son said. "You seem so different; I know he's making you happy these days. I've not seen you like this, ever." It warmed my heart to know that Mark understood so much; he truly was a blessing to me. I told him I wanted him and his brother to meet Eric. He agreed and, after discussion with Brad, we set a dinner date.

We all met at a German restaurant. It was uncomfortable, to say the least. Eric was the total opposite of anyone that my boys imagined or wanted me to be with. He was right-wing in his politics, military-like in his demeanor and clearly uncomfortable as well. We made the best of it, got through it and moved on.

The next day, Mark confided in me. "Mom, who is this man? And why do you want to be with him? He seems so wrong for you."

"I see him for what he is, who he is and what he will be. Trust me, Mark, I wouldn't be with him and investing my time and heart where I didn't think it would be best for me," I told him.

"It's just that I imagined a man that would be head over heels for you. And everyone in the room would know it by the way he acted when he was with you," he said, clearly worried that I was making a huge mistake. "He just seems like a 'cold fish' to me, not the warm, affectionate man I imagined for you".

"Mark, last night, he acted like what he felt was appropriate around my children. I am sure he wasn't certain of how to act around you guys. He doesn't know what you would consider OK and not OK. There's so much to this situation. His wife is 'technically' still living, and he's sitting in a restaurant with young men, wondering how they're judging him for that part of the equation alone. So he erred on the side of caution. I realize that I haven't known him for quite a month yet, but I know him well enough to believe that he wouldn't want anyone to think he wasn't acting like a gentleman with your mother."

"I trust you, Mom, really I do. I trust that you are watching out for you and what you need. And like I said before, you are the happiest

I have seen you, ever. So something must be right," he said as he hugged me.

"Just keep an open mind, Mark. I want you to know the man I know. It will take time, but give him a chance," I told him as we embraced.

In fact, it took a lot longer than I had ever expected, but all of my children have their own relationship and respect for Eric that grows every day. This is more than I could have hoped for, in light of how I handled things. To this day, they know that he is not politically, emotionally or fundamentally like them at all, and not who they imagined their mother to be life partners with. They may not agree with him and wouldn't have picked him out for me, but they came to love the man that was making their mom's life so wonderful.

CHAPTER 8
MEETING GAYE AND THE FAMILY

The day after my conversation with Mark, Eric said, "I'd like you to go to the nursing home with me today. To meet Gaye, that is."

"Of course I'll go. I'd love to go with you," I told him, not thinking about what impression the staff might get as a result.

As we drove up to the facility, I did think about it. How would the staff judge me? I was the "other woman." They didn't know anything about Eric's life except that his wife was in a nursing home. They didn't think about him sitting at home, all alone, day after day—alone until I'd come along. They didn't know of the reckless behavior he had been exhibiting up until I met him. Many times, he rode his motorcycle after having beer at the pub with his friends, and he never monitored his blood sugar. Mel has often confided in me that she felt her father was on a path of self-destruction. The staff didn't know any of these things. They wouldn't even know that now he had joy in his life, happiness in his heart and a smile on his face. All they knew was that he was walking into the facility where his wife lived—–and he was with another woman.

I nervously looked at Eric as we walked down the hall, purposely avoiding eye contact with anyone. We went to her room; a woman walked up behind us and informed us that Gaye was in the TV room.

As we walked into the room, I knew her without Eric having to point her out. She looked like the pictures I had seen, but much frailer and a bit older.

While the skin on her face was young and beautiful, her body told a different story. Since she was facing our way, I could see that she still had her beautiful blue eyes. How could Eric not have gotten lost in them, all those years ago? As we walked further into the TV room, Eric finally spotted her. We then made our way over to the frail, graying blonde woman, sitting all alone in her wheelchair. Her arms, hands and legs were contractured. Her eyes met his and she mumbled. It seemed to me that her eyes might have recognized him but her brain couldn't wrap around the idea of how to respond. She seemed to meet everyone's eyes that way, even mine. He tried to engage her, but she was not able. As we pulled up chairs to sit with her, Eric's demeanor changed.

It was at that moment that I saw the caretaker in him as he reached out to touch his wife. "Hi Gaye," he said as he took a seat in front of her, "hey, hey Gaye." Her eyes seemed to light up a bit as she mumbled some incoherent words. "I have your juice for you. Here, Gaye, drink your juice," he told her in a beautifully sweet voice.

I sat there and admired the love and compassion he had for his wife. Patiently putting the bottle of juice to her mouth for her to drink; wiping the juice that dribbled down her chin. It was a scene right out of a love story—the kind of love that didn't see the shell of who she used to be, but who she was to him. I counted myself blessed to have witnessed such a beautiful scene. We left after a little while and, as we walked down the hall, Eric broke down.

He sobbed as if he had never been allowed to cry before. I held him in my arms and comforted him, sobbing myself. At that point, I didn't care who thought what about who I was. I was there for Eric,

I was there for me, and I was there for the family. It was also at this point that I realized that I was also there for Gaye. My role was clearly defined to me at that moment, so I didn't care what it looked like to anyone. I was meant for this role, and whether I was I born or nurtured into it didn't matter. Who I am made me the perfect candidate, and I embraced both my role here and the people it affected.

I saw a sweet, caring, compassionate side of Eric that night. How could I not embrace Gaye? The man I was in love with had love so deep for her that how could I not love her as well? How could I not fall even more deeply in love with this man who was loyal beyond most? I didn't care what anyone thought, not anymore.

A couple of days later, I was to meet Ila, Gaye's mother. Mel was extremely close to her grandmother and wanted her to meet the woman who was finally bringing joy into her dad's life. I was scared to death! It was a strange enough situation the way it was, and now I had to meet Gaye's mother. No one asked me what I wanted. It was just decided. Ila was coming from Idaho Falls and I was to meet her. If I were asked, would I have gone? Absolutely. Tami does what is asked—even to the detriment of herself—which was why my son worried about my reasons for being with Eric. Not knowing how Ila would react to me, I asked Amanda to attend the lunch at which we were to meet. I needed support. Amanda was only ten, but I knew that having her there would make me feel on more familiar "turf."

It went much better than I had expected. Conversation came easily, and Ila was very open and accepting. After the lunch, she hugged me and said, "I never, in a million years, dreamed that this would happen to my daughter. I am so glad that you're here to help Eric be happy. He deserves it. Thank you."

She seemed to be in a good place, accepting the consequences of her daughter's illness. Her words to me were so sweet and encouraging. She even stayed with us at Eric's house on the final day of her trip. It was a bit uncomfortable, but I embraced her and the situation, trying to ease her pain as best I could. Later on that day, Mel called me and explained that they went to the nursing home after we had lunch. Her grandmother had broken down and told Mel then that she couldn't, and wouldn't, visit Gaye again. It was too painful to see the state her daughter was in. I can only imagine her emotions that day. It's one thing to lose your parent, but to lose a child is almost unbearable in itself; and to lose a child to Alzheimer's has to create even more disturbing emotions than usual in this situation.

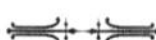

It wasn't long after the meeting with Ila that Eric and I planned a dinner with his brother, Don, and his wife, Madlyn, so that I could meet them. Conversation at the restaurant was going well, and I didn't feel the least bit nervous, until Madlyn said something that made me worry.

"So, Tami, how old are you, exactly?" she asked.

"Forty-four," I told her.

"Why, you're just a 'spring chicken,'" she said. Knowing the Madlyn as I do now, I understand that she didn't mean anything by it, but at the time I felt that she thought I was too young for Eric. He is ten years older than I am, and Madlyn and Don are even older. Would she try to persuade Eric that I was too young for him, and that he should be with someone closer to his own age? I enjoyed the conversation and getting to know them both, but in the back of my mind, I was still thinking about the age comment.

On the drive home, sitting next to Eric in the truck, I expressed my concerns. "Madlyn thinks I'm too young for you," I told him.

"What?" he asked.

"She asked me how old I was, and when I told her, she said, 'Why, you're just a "spring chicken."' Do you think I'm too young for you?" I asked, worried at what his answer might be.

"I think you are just what I needed—a 'spring chicken' to get this old rooster out living his life again. So, no, I do not think you are too young for me," he said as he put his arm around me and hugged me tight. "Don't worry anymore about it. I love my 'spring chicken'!" He said as he smiled. I guess until that night, I hadn't thought about our age difference that much; ten years can be a lot, but not at this time in our lives. It never became an issue for me again, except when Madlyn would bring it up.

It wasn't until later that I learned how close Gaye and Madlyn were. As exceptionally fond sisters-in-law, they had shared their lives, children and intimate moments with one another. When I learned of this, I understood that Madlyn was dealing with the situation in her own way. She was perhaps protecting her feelings and relationship with her sister-in-law, or maybe just protecting Gaye. Either way, once I had affirmation from Eric that he didn't think I was too young for him, that was all I needed.

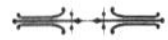

So much had happened that it seemed like I had lived a lifetime in a few weeks. By Thanksgiving, I was pretty much living at Eric's—not officially, but I was always there. As Thanksgiving neared, I found out that I had to work at the hospital, so Eric went to Mel's house for the holiday dinner.

Later, after Thanksgiving, Mel told me that she had been contemplating a discussion with her father about his current living situation and new relationship. After dinner, the boys got up from the table, leaving Jamie, Mel and Eric to clear the dishes away. This, Mel thought, was the perfect opportunity to talk to her dad.

"Dad, it seems like you and Tami are becoming serious kind of quick, don't you think?" she finally asked her father as they began to rinse dishes.

"Yes and no," he told her. "Yes, it's serious, but no, I don't think it's kind of quick. I mean, it's become a lot of things in a short amount of time. But it's right, Mel; it's right and that's all that matters."

"I'm not saying it's not right, I just don't want you to be hurt, that's all" she said with concern on her face.

Eric wrapped his arm around Mel as they stood over the sink, "Mel, you have been after me to find someone to share my life with. I've found her. You like her and I'm sure when Rix meets her, he will too. I'm not going to be hurt. I am happy, happier than I have been in a long time. Don't worry about me; no one is supposed to worry about me," he told her.

"Dad, I hate it when you say that. I will worry about you; it's my job. And you're right about Tami—I do like her. We all do; Grandma adored her. She hugged Eric's neck. "I couldn't have picked anyone better for you myself," she said in his ear as they embraced. "I really am very happy for you."

CHAPTER 9
CHRISTMAS!

I am, have been, and always will be crazy about Christmas. It's my favorite holiday and I have always decorated every nook and cranny of my home. The only difference this year was that I wasn't quite sure where I would decorate. I so wanted to decorate Eric's home, as I wanted him to feel Christmas the way I feel it.

As Christmas neared, I feared that Eric would think I was insane when he saw the amount of Christmas decorations I owned. Tim hated that I had so much and actually resented my Christmas spirit. I had hopes and dreams of meeting a man who would share my spirit or, at the very least, appreciate it. One day, I decided to approach Eric about my ideas.

"Christmas is coming soon and I'd like to decorate the house if it's OK," I said to him one Friday evening.

"Sure, hon, whatever you want. It will be good to have Christmas in here again." He looked around the somewhat bare room.

"But I have to warn you," I said, "I have a lot of Christmas stuff."

"Yes, and I have some too, in the basement. Looks like we'll have a lot together," he said and smiled at me.

"I don't know if you understand—"

"Hon, really, however you want to do it is fine. I'm excited to see it all," he interrupted. "Don't worry about it—I can't wait!" he said.

The following Sunday afternoon, I borrowed Eric's truck and went to Tim's place to retrieve the load of decorations that I had left stored there. I spent almost two hours loading plastic box after plastic box of Christmas decorations onto the truck. Tim was a great help; after all, he was finally getting rid of what to him was just clutter.

"Tell Eric I feel sorry for him now that he has to put up with this stuff," he said with a chuckle. Little did Tim know that I found that to be hurtful. Of course I knew that he hated my Christmas stuff, but he didn't have to remind me of all the painful Christmases I had spent, knowing he was trying to kill my spirit. His words also made me worry that perhaps when Eric saw how much I actually had, he might feel the same way that Tim did.

As I pulled into the driveway, I began to feel anxious. I sat in the truck for a few moments, contemplating how to get rid of a few boxes so it wouldn't look like so much. In the end, I decided that I needed to be me, and that included my Christmas spirit. I came in the door with two boxes stacked on top of each other, grunting and groaning as I entered.

"Oh, hon!" Eric exclaimed. "Let me help you with that." He took a box, and we set both boxes down in the dining room.

"There's more, in the cab of the truck," I told him. We both went out and took the remaining three boxes out of the cab.

After we set them down next to the others, he exclaimed, "This is a lot!"

"This isn't all of it; the truck bed is full of more boxes," I admitted, afraid of what his reaction would be.

"Let's go get them," he said without even batting an eye. A half hour later we were standing in the dining room looking at stacks of boxes. But I wasn't done yet. There were still Eric's decorations to be added to the pile.

He led me into the basement and we brought up a few boxes of tree decorations and a prized Santa collection that was Gaye's. Once we had everything in the dining room, I said, "OK, I have the next three days off. That will give me a great start!"

"Start? How long will this take you?" he asked.

"Usually it takes me a week or so, and with your stuff and a new house to decorate, it may take longer,"

"I can't wait to see it! It's going to be great!" he said—and actually sounded like he meant it.

Day after day, I sifted through the decorations, combining his with mine. It was so magical to see how everything came together. I had saved Gaye's Santas for last. I put them all in the wall niches in the living room. The lights I put in the niches made the room look magical; it was a beautiful tribute to her collection. I heard the garage door open just as I was admiring all my hard work. I met Eric at the door.

"I'm finished!" I exclaimed as I ran to meet him. "It took me almost a week and a half, but I'm done. Come see!"

I led him into the kitchen where there were snowmen on top of every cabinet with lighted "snow" beneath them. There were Christmas dishes in the cupboards along with Christmas glasses and cups. I had serving bowls and trays on the countertops and seasonal magnets on the fridge. I then led him into the living room where there were more snowmen on every window sill and along the stairs. I had draped holiday blankets on the couch and chairs, and doilies on the side tables and coffee table; hanging above the fireplace were stockings, one with each grandchild's name on it, as well as one for Amanda.

Then he saw it—the Santa display.

"That looks so nice, hon," he said with a catch in his voice. "It's beautiful how you put them here. Gaye would have loved it."

We stood there admiring them as he described where some of the more special ones came from. I could see the memories coming back to him and, by asking him questions about the ones he hadn't singled out, I encouraged him to keep remembering. I loved that the display brought back so much to him. To me, that's what Christmas is about—the memories we create with our loved ones—and I was touched to be sharing Eric's memories. I wanted the memories that Gaye had once held dear, and those of her family, to be with us this Christmas. She could no longer be with the family, so I would bring her here as best I could.

As Eric finished his stories, I showed him where I thought the tree should go, and he agreed. I then took him to all the rooms that I had decorated. Even though I had a lot of Christmas stuff, it wasn't enough to fill the house completely, but every room had some Christmas in it. I paid close attention to Amanda's room. This would be her first Christmas with her parents divorced, and I wanted to make it as special as I could. I had taken extra pains to make her room look as though she, herself, had decorated it. I couldn't wait for her to see it!

"When are we going to get our tree?" Eric asked as we came down the stairs after looking at everything.

"I'm off this weekend and have Amanda; we could get it then so that she can help us decorate it," I told him.

"That sounds perfect!" he said. "Did you find out if you work Christmas or Christmas Eve?"

"Christmas Day," I told him. "Which really isn't so bad. Because I'm in the ED that day and don't work until eleven, so we'll have the day before Christmas Eve, Christmas Eve and Christmas morning. Eric's parents were going to be in town and I would be meeting them for the first time. Madlyn, Don, their children, Mel and her family, my children and even Rix and his family, whom I hadn't met yet, would also be coming. I planned to have everyone over for dinner on Christmas Eve and could hardly contain my excitement. It was going to be a great holiday!

Rix and family arrived early so we could get the introductions over with. I met him, Emily, their daughter, Megan, and their then three-year-old son. It felt a bit awkward, but as we moved into the living room, conversation began and we became more comfortable. Megan seemed distant, sitting on the end of the couch, trying not to participate. I didn't quite understand what it was about; I just thought it might be shyness. I soon announced I had dinner to finish up and excused Amanda and myself to the kitchen where we were finishing up the preparations. Emily picked Brian up and took him around the house on a "tour," as she called it, to see all the decorations. Eric and his son stood in the dining room, catching up. Megan stayed on the couch.

As Amanda and I busied ourselves in the kitchen, Megan made the effort to come in and ask if she could be of some help. I promptly took the opportunity to get to know her better and gave her some tasks. The ice seemed to be melting and we had a good time getting acquainted.

It wasn't long before the doorbell rang; it was Mel's family. Jamie, being in retail, couldn't make it on Christmas Eve and wasn't with them. Eric promptly took Mel to see the Santa display, and I stood back to let him share it with her. Her eyes began to tear up. Eric put his arm around her as she began to cry. "This just brings back so many memories," I heard her tell her father.

"I know, but they're good memories, Mel," he said as he held her close to him. It was a tender moment, and I was glad that they were able to share warm Christmas memories of Gaye and their family. Mel called Rix over to the display. "Look, Ricky, look at all of Mom's Santas," she said.

"They look really great, Dad," he told his father.

"Tami arranged them, and I think it all looks perfect," he said as he reached out for my hand. I gave him my hand and gave him a little squeeze to let him know I loved him; then I excused myself to the kitchen so they could share in their memories without me. It was such a beautiful moment in the midst of what was a difficult time of year for them all. But I hoped to help them keep their fond memories of Gaye, and watching them reminisce gave me peace. The three of them looking at the display of Santas brought Gaye to the celebration.

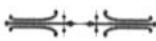

Dinner went well, and I met a few more family members: Eric's parents and his niece and nephew. The table in the dining room wasn't large enough for everyone to fit, so I had set up a buffet. I had arranged seating in the living room, as well as seating in the breakfast nook and at the bar for the grandkids.

After I made sure that everyone had filled their plates, I served myself and ventured into the dining room to take a seat next to Eric. There weren't any empty seats next to him or anywhere at the table, for that matter. Mel, Megan, Rix, Emily, and Eric's parents sat around the table with Eric at the head seat. Realizing there wasn't a place for me, I quietly took my plate back into the living room and took a seat next to Madlyn. I would be lying if I said I didn't feel hurt, but I understood. I was so new to this environment and to this family that, of course, no one would realize that there needed to be a seat for me.

We all, including my children, enjoyed great conversation. After dinner and an exchange of gifts, the family began to leave a few at a time. While seeing Mel and her family off, she hugged me for a long time and said softly in my ear, "Thank you for all of this; we needed it so much. And the Santa display was wonderful; you are so sweet. My dad isn't the only lucky person to have you—we all are." It was a sentiment that I will never forget. She seemed to understand my mission of bringing her mom to Christmas.

As we parted from our embrace, I said, "I wanted your mother here in all of your hearts and minds; I'm happy you sensed the idea." She smiled and I closed the door behind them.

Eric turned to me, announcing, "And a good time was had by all!"

I agreed and felt the warm glow of Christmas linger through the air as we walked, hand in hand, into the dining room to clear away the last desert dishes.

"You're quite the hostess," Eric said as we took the dishes into the kitchen.

"It was all so fun, especially because it's Christmas," I said as I began to fill up the sink with soapy water. "Mel thanked me for including Gaye; I just hope Rix also understood my motivation for putting his mother's things out. I didn't know if I should have talked to him about it, because we had just met," I explained.

"He understood and he loved it," Eric reassured me.

As we finished doing the dishes, Eric sat on the couch and motioned for me to sit next to him. "I was just thinking about the dinner table. Mom and Dad were to my right; Mel, Megan, and Emily were to my left; and Rix was at the other end. Where did you eat?" he asked.

"Oh, I sat in the living room with everyone else. It was nice getting to know everyone," I told him.

"Oh, I guess I expected you to sit with me," he said, sounding a bit hurt.

"I wanted to, but everyone had begun eating and looked so comfortable in their seats that I didn't want anyone to move for me," I explained.

"You should have been in the dining room with me, though," he said. "I'm sorry I didn't save a seat for you; how insensitive of me."

"Don't worry about it. You were with your family; perhaps it was how it needed to be," I said as I snuggled close in to his body while he wrapped his arms around me. "I love the glow of Christmas, can't you feel it?" I asked softly.

"Yes," he said with a satisfied sigh, "it's been a long time since I have felt it and I have you to thank for that. I love you, Tami," he said softly.

"I love you too, Eric," I said as I lifted my head to give him a gentle kiss. It wasn't the first time we had professed loving each other, but it was the most endearing "I love you" I had ever heard. I laid my head back on his chest as we hugged each other tight. While he kissed my head, thoughts of Gaye and her family were in my mind and heart. I knew I was where I was supposed to be, not only because I needed and wanted to be with Eric, but because I also needed and wanted to be with his family as well. I wanted to help them with this journey that they were taking with their dear loved one. I sensed that they all needed guidance to help deal with the pain and loss. I wasn't an expert, but I would do my best to make the journey a memorable one that would bring Gaye joy as well as peace.

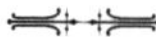

CHAPTER 10

UNLOCKING THE PAIN

In the following weeks, Eric seemed to go to the nursing home even less than before. Concerned about why he wasn't visiting Gaye, I decided to ask him about it when he got home one night.

When Eric sat down on his chair after coming home from work, I sat next to him in the rocking chair that was quickly becoming "my chair" and I asked him, "Did you go see Gaye today?"

"No, I was real busy today," he replied.

I got up and sat myself in his lap. "Eric, I'd like to know why you haven't been going to see her lately. I want you to know it doesn't bother me in the least that you go. As a matter of fact, I love that you visit her and it's bothering me that you're doing it less often than before."

"No, no hon, it doesn't have anything to do with you. It's just that it's getting so painful to see her like this. She's not the Gaye I knew; she doesn't even look the same. Lately her looks have changed even more. It's just so painful," he said as he fought back tears.

I put my arms around him and held him tight. "I'm so sorry, honey. I guess I didn't realize. Though I didn't know Gaye, if I were in her shoes, I guess I would tell you to take care of you and do what you need to do to get through this."

He nodded his head as tears rolled down his cheeks.

"Would you mind if I went to visit Gaye from time to time? I just want to make sure she is taken care of properly and that her needs are met," I asked him, breaking the silence.

"No, of course not," he said with a surprised look on his face.

"I know I said I liked going with you to support you, but if you're unable to go down there anymore, I'd like to visit in your stead," I explained.

"I love that idea. You really are too good to me," he said with a smile.

"It seems like it's been a while since you've been down there. I'd like to run down there now, before dinner, if that's OK," I said.

"Sure, I'll go down there with you," he said.

The drive was quiet. Eric seemed to be gathering his inner strength for the visit. As we approached Gaye, sitting in the dining room, we each took a seat in front of her. Eric offered her the juice he had brought. Gaye's eyes seemed to dart from Eric's face to mine. At that moment, I felt that Gaye was "there" and understood who I was to her husband. It sent a chill down my spine, to say the least. As she made eye contact with me, she seemed to try to get out of her wheelchair. Gaye had been wheelchair bound since she broke her hip a year and a half ago; for her to attempt to stand would be a monumental and fruitless task.

Many family members had told me that Gaye had a jealous streak as deep as the Grand Canyon. When it came to Eric, she wouldn't tolerate any woman even looking at her husband, much less sitting next to him. I understood what she was telling me. I promptly moved to a chair behind her, out of her sight. From that moment on, I decided that, in the future, if I were ever there with Eric, I would stay out of Gaye's line of vision. I wanted nothing but peace and love for her, whether she was "there" or not; whether or not she experienced occasional glimpses of reality, I would not disrespect her ever again by letting her witness me sitting next to her husband.

As Eric and I drove home, he asked me why I had moved away from him. I merely stated that I felt it was disrespectful and that, from what family had told me of her, she would be jealous of me sitting next to him. I left it at that, as I didn't want to give him the idea that perhaps Gaye had flashes of awareness. It horrified me to think that, from time to time, she might realize that she was alone in a nursing home—the place she had never wanted to be, with the disease she had feared the most. I couldn't imagine what that idea would do to Eric and I resolved to keep it to myself.

From then on, I visited Gaye often. I'd sit with her, hold her hand, make sure she was covered up (Eric told me Gaye was usually cold) and tell her about her children and grandchildren. I'd give Eric reports on my visits and sometimes he'd go with me, but not very often.

One sunny afternoon, after a visit with Gaye, I returned home just as Eric arrived from work. After our hug and kiss hello, we moved inside and sat down in our usual chairs.

"You look deep in thought," Eric finally said, breaking the silence.

"I was just wondering about the nursing home. How did you come to choose the one Gaye is at?" I asked him.

"Mel found it. It was so much better than I could have hoped for, after the facility she was in before. Why? Is there something wrong?" he asked.

"No, no, not at all. I think it's a beautiful facility that takes wonderful care of Gaye. I just wondered, I guess. When, exactly, did she go into her first nursing home?" I asked.

"About a year and a half after we came home from Europe." Eric then told me about the nightmare of trying to care for Gaye at home and all he'd had to endure to get her the care she needed. "Watching the emergency technicians take Gaye in the ambulance to go to the hospital was the hardest thing I had ever had to witness, up to that point. It was as if her fears and distrust of me were legitimate. I was having her taken away from her home; so it was as if I *was* out to get her," he explained as the pain of that day seemed to come back to him.

Then he looked at me and said, "But that wasn't the worst day. The worst day was when we transported her to the first nursing home from the hospital. That was a nightmare," he said as his lips began the now familiar quivering when he spoke of painful memories.

"Eric, if it's too painful, you don't have to tell me about it," I said as I reached out to hold his hand to comfort him.

"No, maybe it will help ease the pain if I share it with you," he said as he put his hand in mine. He then began to relive the terrible memory. He spoke of her fears and her pleading for him not to leave her there. It was then that he paused and took a deep breath and said through sobs, "I didn't know what else to do; she was begging me to stay with her. So I did." Eric broke down. It was as if years of emotions were finally let out of a tightly locked box that had been hidden away.

Once he was able to continue, he said, "The thought of Gaye, alone and scared in the nursing home, wrenched my heart from my chest. Every night I stayed with her, I hoped the next one would be better." By this time, Eric was sobbing uncontrollably.

I then got up and motioned him to move to the couch with me. I wrapped my arms around him and tried to ease away some of his distress. The tears kept coming; it was as though he were finally allowing himself to feel the pain of those times.

I could no longer control my emotions either and broke down. "This is so sad; Gaye doesn't deserve this!" I kept telling myself and God. This was cruelly unfair, and Gaye and Eric didn't deserve such suffering.

Eric then shook his head as if to erase the memories. He wiped away his tears and tried to recompose himself, but it was all fruitless.

His sobs became louder and filled with even more pain as he explained, "I cried at the nursing home—I cried for Gaye and everything happening—I felt so foolish, like I do now!"

"Eric," I interrupted, "foolish? Your wife, the mother of your children, the love of your life, was condemned for the rest of her days to a nursing home with a disease that would soon rob her of the memories of all she loved. I know you, and I know you were weeping for Gaye and her sentence. But you were weeping for yourself as well. You lost your life partner and had to make a decision about her care. A decision that no one, ever, wants to make about their loved one, especially when still in the prime of life. There is no foolishness in feeling pain." My own tears were streaming down my face as I spoke.

"I know that ultimately Gaye is the Alzheimer's victim. But you are a victim too. The disease ravages you and the family as well. After a while, Gaye didn't know anything different; she doesn't know she is sick; she really doesn't know much about what is going on at this point. As Alzheimer's has taken over her mind and then her body, she has become unaware; she is perhaps in another place and certainly not 'here.' But you and the rest of the family are still so painfully aware. You've had to witness what the horrific disease was capable of. You are not foolish in your grief; you are well justified to be sad and angry at what it has done and what it will continue to do!"

I sat there holding him, as we both cried. I kept thinking about the pain he'd had to endure, and the pain he would still have to endure. There would be more sad days ahead, I reminded myself, but none, I believed, would be as heartrending as that day when Eric had to leave his beloved behind, both physically and emotionally, in a home that was not theirs.

CHAPTER 11

MOTORCYCLES, EUROPE AND A NEW HOUSE

Life went on. We would spend our weekends doing things with Amanda and riding the motorcycle. The first time I got on the bike with Eric, it was pure joy. Eric had once told me that he'd bought a motorcycle soon after Gaye went into the nursing home. He needed it for a "sort of therapy." He had always wanted a motorcycle but they scared Gaye. The first year he owned one, he put 18,000 miles on it; he said it was like meditation for him and an escape when he was on the bike—he escaped a lot. He went to the Sturgis Bike Rally the first year he owned it and had a great adventure.

I always knew that whomever I would spend the rest of my life with had to have a motorcycle. Tim and I had talked about getting one for years, but we never did. I always knew I wanted to be on the back of one with the man I loved. It was a chilly November day when he took me out for the first time, but I delighted in every moment. He seemed a bit nervous having someone on the back for the first few times, but he soon got used to it and, to this day, we ignore the weather and get on the bike when most people wouldn't dream of even taking a walk.

It was during this time that we talked a lot about going to Europe. Eric wanted me to see and fall in love with the Europe he adored. In fact, a couple of months after we met, Eric was offered a job in Germany again and called to tell me.

"So what do you think?" he asked after he had explained the offer and where it was.

"I think you need to do what you need to do," I said with my heart in my throat. The thought of losing him, after I had just found him, terrified me. But I truly believed he needed to do what was best for him.

"Well, should I take it or not?" he asked.

"Like I said, whatever is best for you," I told him, trying to choke back my tears.

"We could try to find a nursing job for you over there, perhaps on a military base," he said.

"Oh! You mean I would go with you?" I asked, surprised.

"Well, of course," he said, "I wouldn't go without you!"

Relief set in and I gathered my thoughts. "Eric, Amanda has four more years of school until she graduates. I can't possibly leave until then."

"Yeah, I thought you'd say that. OK, then it's decided. I won't take it," he said.

"Anyway, your family is here as well. Would you be able to leave them?" I asked.

"They're grown, they'd be fine," he assured me. In my mind I wondered how he could leave them with their mother in the nursing home. But at the same time, I understood his need to get away from the situation. If he weren't here, he wouldn't have to face the facts of her deteriorating health.

In April the following year, Eric and I took a vacation to Europe. Needless to say, the trip was amazing! I met all of his and Gaye's friends. It was painful for him to explain to them about her health. They were most supportive of Eric and accepted me with open arms. They seemed a bit hesitant about talking of Gaye. I would quickly begin sharing stories that Eric had told me of their lives in Europe, to encourage them to speak freely about her, so that they, too, could remember their dear friend.

I learned about how much they all loved Eric and Gaye; it warmed my heart to know that Eric was reliving happy memories of their lives together. There was a time, or two, that Eric would break down. Going to Sacré Coeur, in Paris, was most painful for Eric. As we walked into the beautiful church, I felt a difference in his demeanor. As I looked up at him, he had tears running down his cheeks. "What is it? What's the matter?" I asked him in a somewhat panicked tone.

"I didn't think it would be so hard." He pressed his lips together to stop them from trembling, and for a moment, he didn't speak. "This was Gaye's favorite place in Europe," he finally said.

Not knowing what else to do, I said, "Let's go, come on." I led him out of the building, and we made our way down the steps and over to an area where there weren't as many people. As we sat down, I asked him, "Why did you bring me here if you knew it was Gaye's favorite place? Didn't you realize how it would affect you?" I asked, angry at myself for sounding like I was scolding him.

He looked at me and said, "I wanted you to see it, it's so beautiful. I didn't want you to miss it just because of me."

"We've seen so much, it would have been fine if we missed it. But I want you to think about why Gaye loved it so much," I told him.

"Because it was beautiful and she said she felt so close to God here," he explained after some thought.

"Then close your eyes and remember. Remember her thrill at being here and the words she used to express her love for this place. Remember all those things—not the sadness you feel because she was once here, but the happiness because she was. Holding on to the good memories may help with the pain," I said, trying to console him.

As he closed his eyes, I could see him go to another place, the place in his memory where he and Gaye were standing in the church. I delighted in the feeling of joy that I was getting from him. Calm came over him; there were still tears, but some were tears of joy. Eric explained that he could see Gaye falling in love with Sacré Coeur and that he felt he was reliving it in his mind for himself and for her.

As he came back from his memory, he opened his eyes and looked at me. "Thank you, you were right. It's just so hard to put things in perspective that way. But remembering the 'happy' is what Gaye would want. Not living in the 'sad' of how things are now. There is still sadness though," he continued, "sadness because she can't remember these things herself," he said as he broke down.

"So you remember for her," I said. "Someday, and I truly believe this, someday when she is free from her body, she will remember Sacré Coeur and everything else that was taken from her. The Bible says we go to heaven whole, and I believe she will have her memories with her. But I feel it is your job to keep them alive for her and for you and for the life you had together. Keep them alive in your heart and mind, and keep them happy."

It was then that Eric looked into my eyes with such a deep, penetrating look that it almost scared me.

"What? What's the matter?" I asked puzzled.

"Where did you come from? How did I get so lucky to have found you? Who sent you to me and why do I deserve you?" he asked with a bewildered look.

"I believe we were sent to be together for numerous reasons. I need to be here for you to help you and your family through your painful journey. I need to be here to help you love again. You were sent to me so that I may experience the most challenging time I will ever face as a nurse and as a human being, and so that I could find myself again. You were sent to me to show me love, the kind of love I've ached for my entire life. We were brought together for each other; this isn't one-sided, Eric. We are both here for each other."

"I'm the luckiest man in the world," he said softly as he wrapped his arms around me. It was truly one of the sweetest moments of my life.

In March, before our trip, I had given up my apartment when my lease was up and moved in "officially" with Eric. He and I spent our days getting to know each other, discussing our past lives, sharing our hopes for the future and discovering a love that was beyond anything I could have imagined. I was the happiest I had ever been and couldn't believe my good fortune.

There were many times when Eric would stumble on a memory of Gaye and I'd try to help him relive the memory, making it a good thing. Tears were shed, but soon Eric became good at storing his happy memories of Gaye instead of turning them into sadness. "Once, I bought Gaye a blouse that she had been wanting for a long time," he said one evening. "At the time, we didn't have much money. We were young and I was still in school. She didn't notice me walk into the bedroom as she was standing in front of the mirror. She was twirling around and dancing around with the blouse on. She loved it! It was the sweetest thing I'd ever seen her do. I stood there, without her knowing, watching her; she was so happy."

"What a wonderful memory, Eric!" I exclaimed. "Keep it there, just like that. Remember her like that, young, pretty and happy with something so simple as a new blouse. Keep that in the front of your mind, always. This is one of the most important memories of her, for you. I think this is how she would want you to remember her," I tutored him.

For all my contentment at this time, I had the occasional qualm that I was still being too much of a nurse to Eric and his situation. On one occasion when this concern had entered my mind, I prayed and meditated about it the whole day and well into the night. The next morning, I woke up early. When I came downstairs and entered the kitchen, I stopped in my tracks as a feeling of déjà vu came over me. Eric, dressed for work in a white shirt and dark tie, was standing at the counter, sipping coffee. He looked impeccable, except that his tie was just a bit crooked.

As I reached up to straighten his tie, I knew. It was just like the dream that I'd recounted to my old friend, Wynne, at the time of my divorce. Only now it was no dream. In real life, I was in a kitchen much like what I'd envisioned, face-to-face with the handsome man in my dream as we exchanged loving looks in a moment of everyday intimacy. I shared my realization with Eric, knowing in my heart of hearts that I was exactly where I belonged.

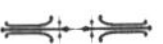

One Saturday afternoon, not long afterward, we were on a motorcycle ride and Eric stopped at a model home. "Let's go in," he said.

We looked at a few houses, and as we looked around the biggest one, Eric asked me, "So what do you think about this house?"

"It's beautiful," I said, "but if I had this house, I'd have to hire someone to clean it, because it's way too much house for me to keep up!"

When we arrived home, I got busy preparing dinner. "Do you like cooking in this kitchen?" Eric asked.

"Of course, it's a very nice kitchen to cook in. But I'd like to make some changes someday, if that's OK," I said.

"What kind of changes?" Eric asked.

"Oh, I'd like darker cabinets, a gas range, double ovens, granite counter tops, stainless steel appliances. Stuff like that," I explained.

"That's a lot of money; we should just buy a new house," he said.

"Is that why you took me to those models today?" I asked.

"Yes, I've been thinking about it for a long time. I know you've been painting and decorating this house to try and make it 'ours,' but the truth is, that this is Gaye's house. She wanted it, so I bought it for her. I'll never forget how excited she was when we found it on the Internet."

He paused for a moment, remembering. "We were still living in Europe and heading back here to find a diagnosis. We had a realtor here in the States and she emailed us some Internet links to homes we might be interested in. The house wasn't quite built yet, but Gaye fell in love with the charm of how it would look. I had my reservations; it backed onto a busy street. I showed Gaye several other houses, trying to get her to change her mind, but she fell in love with this one, and I wanted her to have it. It made me happy that she was so excited." Eric smiled, with tears in his eyes, while he relived the memory. I put my arm around his waist and looked deep into his eyes.

And with tears of my own, I said softly, "Another great memory to hold on to, honey. Remember how happy she was here and how much she loved her house."

With the feeling warming our hearts, he said, "You're right, it is a really great memory. But this is exactly why I think I would like a house that is just 'ours.' What do you think?" he said with a smile.

"I guess, if that's what you want, but Eric, I don't want a house the size of the one we looked at today. I really don't want, nor do I think we need, a house that big," I told him.

"You're right, we'll keep looking. When we find the right one, we'll know," he said.

It was exciting to think of a house that would be "ours." There was nothing wrong with the beautiful home we lived in. It just needed a woman's touch, which I had begun to give it, but Eric was right—we needed one that was just ours, so that this house could always remain Gaye's.

Not too long after our conversation, we found a house that Eric fell in love with. It was beautiful, still much larger than I wanted, but I felt Eric had endured so much pain that he deserved whatever he wanted. We put down a deposit with a contingency on selling the other house; we put it on the market, I staged it as best I could and we waited.

⟿⟾

I've learned that through any journey, everyone has to travel it the way that's best for them. For Eric, it was to move on when he felt the time was right. At the beginning of his nightmare, he wasn't ready, but later—at the urging of his daughter, and with the rest of the family supporting him—he decided that he needed to find some happiness in the midst all his misery. He wondered, in the beginning, if any woman would actually be interested in a man in his situation, not to mention with his health issues. But between the time his dear wife no longer recognized him and the time he decided to start dating again, he did a lot of "soul searching." During this period, according to Mel, he took risks with his health and safety that, whether he was conscious of it or not, endangered his life. He once described to me his life before he met me as "just existing: eating because I needed to, not because I wanted to." Eric moved forward when he felt he was ready and in the way he felt was best for him. Everyone's journey is their own and, in my opinion, no one should ever dictate what is right for anyone else.

There are many ways in which life can, and can't, go on in a situation such as ours. Although Eric wanted to "emotionally" move on, by finding someone to share his life with, he really couldn't do so completely. The fact that Gaye was still living really posed no barrier for either of us, but there were some legal issues that we hadn't thought about. For example, one day during the construction of our new home, I was at work and excitingly talking to another ER nurse about the house that we were having built.

One of the doctors overheard my conversation. "Tami, I hate to butt in but I overheard your conversation about the house you're buying." Dr. Marcus knew of our situation and was a great support to me.

"I don't mean to put a damper on your house plans. But what happens if Eric dies first? You've told me he is diabetic and has had a bypass, so who's to say Eric will outlive his wife? She's young; she could live another ten to twenty years. My concern is that you are putting your own money into this house as well. You've also put your money into the house you're living in now to fix it up to sell; you have your furniture, household goods and even your clothes in your shared home. If Eric dies first, you are out of luck and on the street because she is his wife and will have rights to everything. You will have nothing, nothing to move on with or to start your own life again. In the eyes of the law, you are not entitled to anything, not even what was yours," he counseled.

He was right. What recourse would I have? I was just the "other woman." The state wouldn't care who I was or how much money I spent on the old house or the new house. How would I financially, not to mention emotionally, be able to move on, if Eric were to die before we could marry? I was investing not just my time but the money I had from my divorce on the two homes. The money that was meant for me to buy a place for me and Amanda was going into the houses. I could have nothing left—nothing to move on with.

But how could I talk to Eric about this? How would I tell him that I was in fear of losing my money if he were to die before Gaye? We were partners at this point; we were committed to each other and knew that we wanted to be together forever. I was further committed to the family and to Gaye, but I did need to think about this aspect of our relationship. There were no laws to protect me. Dr. Marcus was right; I had to talk to Eric, as uncomfortable as it might be.

The next day, I decided I needed to put it in front of him. "Honey, there's something that I am finding hard to talk to you about. It has to do with finances," I began. Even though Eric and I had been living together for almost a year, and considered ourselves partners, we had to keep our finances separate due to his marital status. I contributed to the household by taking over certain bills and the groceries. I felt that, as a partner, I should pay my share, but our finances were completely separate.

"What about them?" he asked.

"If you passed away before Gaye does, I am out everything I have put into this house as well as everything I'll be putting into the new house, because the state would give it all to your 'legal' wife," I explained. "What am I supposed to do to get on with my life, if that were to happen? How would I be able to buy a place to live? At this point I have my money in savings that I'll be putting into the new house, but if you were to die after we buy it, I'll be out that money as well as what I have spent here."

"Yes, but there's life insurance money. You'd be able to get your money back from that," he said, trying to come up with a solution.

At that point, I didn't know about any life insurance policies that Eric might have had. This was the first I had heard of it. "Don't you worry," Eric said. I'll take care of this first thing tomorrow, when I get in to the office. Gaye is the beneficiary on the policy that I have. I'll change it to you instead."

"Wait, honey," I pleaded, "I don't know how much the policy is, but all I need is what I've put into the houses, so I could start a new life. Your children deserve their share," I said as tears filled my eyes.

"Why are you tearing up?" Eric asked.

"The thought is horrifying to me. I hate even entertaining the idea of losing you," I told him.

"Oh hon," he said as he wrapped his arms around me, "I'm not going anywhere. You're stuck with me for the 'long haul.' But don't worry. I'll take care of the insurance policy. I wish I'd thought about this a long time ago; I'm so glad you said something. I would roll over in my grave if I thought for one moment I would leave you penniless."

The next day, Eric brought home paperwork for me to fill out and sign. After signing the papers, I looked up at him. "Eric, promise me I'll have thirty years with you, and that there's no need for the insurance policy," I said with tears rolling down my cheeks.

"I promise, at least thirty years!" he assured me and hugged me tight.

CHAPTER 12

THE "BIG" GIFT

Our second Christmas was approaching and we were busy with the usual Christmas planning and gift buying. Eric kept pestering me to tell him what it was I wanted for Christmas. I truly felt I had everything I needed and couldn't give him a clue because I, myself, didn't know. Eric then surprised me, two weeks before Christmas, with my Christmas gift. He called me on his drive home telling me he would be home early. Excited about seeing him two hours earlier than usual, I tidied up my face and waited for him to get home. He came in the garage door as usual. He looked excited, worried and, possibly, as though his blood sugar was crashing, I wasn't able to tell which it was.

Within a few weeks of knowing Eric, I had been able to tell when his blood sugar was too low; he gets a specific look on his face when it happens. I've never been wrong about it and can usually make a pretty accurate estimate as to how low his blood sugar actually is. This day was no different, but I sensed that excitement was also playing a part.

A quick hug and kiss, and I was off to the kitchen to get the juice he needed to elevate his blood sugar. He went to the bedroom to put away his badge and things for the evening. I took the juice to him there.

He gulped it down and then said, "I got your Christmas present today." He looked as though he might explode if he didn't tell me.

"Oh really, so…what is it?" I said jokingly, knowing he would never ruin my surprise by telling me.

"I'm thinking of giving it to you today," he continued, "but I don't want to because I wanted to wait until Christmas. But it's big, it's really big!" he exclaimed as he walked back into the foyer.

The first thought in my mind was, "He's bought a washer and dryer for the new house!" He kept saying it was big, really big, so of course I thought he meant the size of the gift was big. "If it's that big, how are you going to keep it hidden? You might as well give it to me; besides, if you don't, I think you're going to explode!" I told him.

He looked at me with those beautiful excited green eyes and then turned to get something from his jacket hanging in the hallway. As he took the item from his jacket pocket, I assumed he was getting his keys so he could take me to the truck to see the gift. But then he turned to face me and fell to one knee. I, nurse that I am, recalled his blood sugar dropping earlier and thought he was too weak to move.

"Eric!" I shouted, "Are you OK? What's the matter?"

He looked up at me, pulled a ring box from behind his back, took my hand and asked, in a sweet but shaky voice, "When we can, will you marry me?"

I couldn't believe what I had just heard! We had discussed marriage and knew it was what we wanted. But our circumstances dictated how and when we would be able to be married, so I had put the idea on the back burner for the time being. Eric, being the kind of man he was, would never divorce his beloved wife just so he could get married, nor would I ever ask that of him. It was one of his traits that I admired the most. When Eric said "till death do us part," he meant it. For him to ask me to marry him "when we can" was a shock to me, to say the least.

I began crying at once. I didn't need to answer—he knew I'd marry him—but I finally uttered, "Yes, of course I will!" We embraced and held each other for a few moments.

He put the ring on my finger and we kissed and embraced again. It was just us in this moment; nothing or anyone else existed but us.

Once the excitement and adrenaline started to fade, I became painfully aware of what his children might say. After all, their mother was still living. Was this the right thing to do? I wondered out loud.

"What?" Eric asked. "What did you just say?"

"Is this the right thing to do? Your children may not approve. They may think we should have waited to do this," I explained to him.

"I don't care what they'll think or say. Years ago, they told me to move on. When I was finally able to do so, I found you, the angel sent to help me heal and to find love again. I am healing and this is part of the process for me. I need the promise of a happy day, the day you'll be my wife," he explained as he looked at the beautiful ring on my finger.

As we sat on the couch, I contemplated how to tell his children. My kids would be excited and happy for me, but they weren't in the same situation as Eric's kids were. I decided to tell Melanie first. She and I had become close over the past year, and I knew it would be easier for me to tell her than anyone else in the family. I took a picture of the ring on my hand with my phone and nervously hit the send button. I knew she would be busy studying; she had started prerequisites for nursing school that fall and was a busy student as well as a bread earner and mother for her family. I thought a text message that she could look at in her own time would be the easiest way to tell her. As I pressed the send button, my heart was pounding in my chest; I waited for a text message back. Instead, the phone rang. I looked up at Eric. "Uh-oh, she's calling me. I wonder if she'll be upset."

"Answer it and see what she says," he said as he looked at the phone in my hand.

"I'm afraid," I told him.

"Don't be silly, just answer it," he said.

I finally accepted the call and heard a very excited Mel on the other end. "Is that what I think it is?" she yelled.

"If you think it's an engagement ring, then yes, it is," I said, with my heart now in my throat.

"Whoooooo hooooo!!!! I am so excited, I'm jumping up and down on my bed! I've been waiting for this to happen!" she said in her typical enthusiastic Melanie fashion. Her excitement fuelled my own. "The boys are excited too! I just told them; we are all so happy!" she continued.

"I was a bit afraid to tell you; I didn't know how you'd feel about it," I said.

"It really didn't matter how I felt about it, and to tell you the truth, it doesn't matter what anyone thinks! Tami, you have brought so much joy into my dad's life. This is just another way for him to move on and get past the nightmare he has to live every day while my mom's still here. You have brought him hope, joy and love while still keeping my mom's memory alive and important to him. You've helped us all, in your own way, and you've brought our dad back to us. With this promise of the future, you'll be a part of this family 'officially' when it's the right time."

Whew! Melanie was not only OK with it, but ecstatic! But what about Rix? I wondered. How would he feel?

Eric decided that he would call his son to tell him. "Hey Rix, I just gave Tami her Christmas gift bit early." He paused and then revealed the news of our engagement. After the brief phone call, Eric hung up with a smile. "Rix said to tell you that he is happy for us both," he informed me.

Melanie was right. Whether anyone else in the world, thought we were wrong didn't matter. Eric needed to move on with his life, and if this helped him deal with it, then so be it. I was excited, to say the least, and relieved that his family approved.

As Christmas approached, my thoughts turned to Gaye, even more than usual. There was, again, no way could she be here for Christmas, physically, so I once more put out the Santa arrangement so that she would be lovingly remembered by all of us. One afternoon, I took a poinsettia to her, sat with her as she lay in her bed, and softly sang a few Christmas songs to her. I don't know if she understood anything I was doing, but I wanted to share the spirit of Christmas with her as best I could.

I wouldn't be telling the truth if I said I didn't receive anything from the visit, because I did. I filled myself with as much of her spirit as she would let me. As I sat there, I thought of Eric's stories of Gaye's Santas—how she acquired them, where she got them and why they were special to her. I pictured the Santas in their illuminated niches at home and spoke of them softly to her. She didn't respond, but I hoped that, perhaps, she was in a place where she was enjoying what I was sharing with her. Once my heart was full and I was sure that Gaye was comfortable, I gathered my things, kissed her forehead and headed home. I truly felt blessed sharing that time with her. I don't know how to describe it, but it felt as though we had a bond between us. Perhaps it was a figment of my imagination, but I liked the feeling and would hold on to it forever. As we all gathered for Christmas, I was mindful of Gaye so that the part of her spirit she'd shared with me was there with us.

CHAPTER 13
DIFFICULT DECISIONS

The house finally sold in February of the following year, and we moved into our new home in March 2009—during a blizzard! We had fought for so long and so hard to have this day that we were determined to sleep in our new home whether the weather wanted us to or not. Though the house still seemed larger than I'd ever wanted, I loved it because Eric did. He was in heaven!

But there remained a lingering sadness on a day-to-day basis. Gaye was always in our thoughts. We talked about her often and looked at pictures of her. I would always ask Eric to explain the picture and the memory associated with it. Some times were tougher than others, but I always tried to make the memories good ones that Eric could cherish forever and reflect on when he needed them.

In July of that year, Eric was with me on one of my visits to Gaye. "She's losing weight," I thought to myself. I didn't want to alarm Eric and kept the thought to myself. Eric didn't accompany me on very many visits anymore, which, it would seem, would make her weight loss more apparent to him. But it didn't.

On another visit in late September, with Eric joining me again, I finally told him what I was observing. "She's lost a lot of weight lately, don't you think?" I whispered to him as we looked at her sleeping peacefully on her bed.

That's the thing about this disease. In all the times I had visited Gaye over the past two and a half years, I had never thought she was in pain. The disease seemed to be a silent killer, starting by killing memories, then moving to bodily functions. I take comfort in knowing that she never seemed be the slightest bit uncomfortable. The nursing staff were such angels and took painstaking measures to make sure that Gaye was comfortable at all times. She was always clean, bathed, and nicely dressed, with her hair combed. In my opinion, the painful part of the disease, for an Alzheimer's patient, is the initial realization of having the disease, before inevitably becoming "unaware." But one's comfort in knowing that the person with Alzheimer's isn't "aware" is soon replaced by the pain of watching the disease take your loved one, bit by bit. Robbing people of their mind and memories isn't enough for Alzheimer's. It wants the body as well and flaunts its power so that everyone can see the destruction, as if it reveled in everyone's pain.

"You really think the weight loss is that pronounced?" Eric asked.

"I'm sure of it," I told him.

"Let's go talk to the nurse," he said as he motioned for me to follow him out of the room. We approached the nurses' station and Eric asked for Gaye's records; we discovered she had lost seventeen pounds. When we voiced our concerned to the nurse on duty, she informed him that the "care team" was in the process of setting up a care conference soon and would contact him when they could get it scheduled. Although by this time the nurses knew me and treated me respectfully, they wouldn't discuss such things with me. I totally understood; it would be a HIPPA violation. So I never asked. It was only when Eric was with me that I would be able to ask my own questions, medical as well as non-medical. I looked forward to the conference.

A week later, Eric and I met with the care team to discuss the issue of Gaye's weight loss. Eric introduced me to the team members that didn't know me yet and we all sat down. "Gaye is eating only pureed foods at this time," Ellen, the Care Team Coordinator, began the discussion. "She seems to finish about 75 to 100 percent of her meals, but she continues to lose weight. We are having the dietician assess how to fortify her food to prevent her from losing any more," she explained. "But, Mr. Reeves, the issue at hand is this: More than likely, Gaye may start refusing her oral intake. In the event, we need you to tell us whether you want a feeding tube placed to keep her fed."

Eric looked to me for an explanation. I gently said, "It's a tube placed in her nose down into her stomach, or a permanent fixture could be placed on her stomach so they can access her stomach with a tube." I motioned with my hands to indicate where the imaginary tube would be on my stomach. "That way they can feed her pureed nutrition. The tube that goes through the nose is uncomfortable putting it in, the first time. But once in place, the patient doesn't notice it much after a while. I am sure they wouldn't subject her to surgery for the other kind of feeding tube, but that they would use the one that goes in the nose. Am I correct?" I asked Ellen. She nodded yes.

"What do you think, hon?" he asked me with tears in his eyes and fear on his face.

"Eric, this is a discussion you need to have with your children. You shouldn't make this decision on your own and my opinion doesn't matter here. It's what you and the kids feel is in Gaye's best interest," I explained to him.

Eric turned to the care team, the slight quiver in his lips signaling his distress as he spoke: "I need to talk this over with my kids. Can I get back to you in a day or two?"

As the care conference continued, we learned that if Gaye had been in her eighties, she would have passed away by now. But she was only in her mid-fifties. Who would have guessed that having a young healthy body could be a bad thing for anyone? Apparently, it is no boon for an Alzheimer's patient. Gaye's young body kept her imprisoned longer than anyone wanted, family members especially.

The care team mentioned the possible eventual need for IV hydration as well. I explained to Eric that if Gaye wasn't taking in nutrition or fluids by the placement of a feeding tube, she'd become dehydrated. Not being an end-of-life nurse, I asked about the pain, if any, of dying of dehydration. We were given a pamphlet on death from dehydration as well as a pamphlet on end-of-life symptoms. Eric, fighting back tears, once again told the team that he would let them know after he spoke to Mel and Rix.

We left that day with sad hearts. While we all wanted Gaye to be free of her body, it was difficult to see her like this. Worse still was having to let her go and to make decisions that would ultimately end her life.

Not long before the care conference, Mel had confided in me, "Tami, I told Mom, three years ago, that it was OK for her to go. That she needed to go. I didn't want her to suffer and I never wanted to see her deteriorate as she has. It's painful to watch her go from the beautiful woman I knew as my mom to someone that hardly looks like her. I can't handle seeing her like this; it kills me every time I do."

"Mel, it's the beautiful woman you remember that you need to hold on to," I tried to console her. "You may see your mom in much worse shape. Just hold on to the memories you have of her and not to what you'll be witnessing as she nears the end of her battle. Just remember the mom who's in your heart."

The family was now faced with Gaye's rapid deterioration and, with it, the painful end-of-life decisions that had to be made. The difficulty for Eric was that he now faced having to discuss these decisions with his children. How does a father talk to his children about what they should and shouldn't do to prolong their dear mother's battle and to be rid of her body? It was a sensitive subject, but one that they had all known they would have to deal with when they received the diagnosis all those years ago.

⁂

Once at home, Eric again asked what I thought about the tube feedings as well as the IV hydration.

"First, I think you need to read these pamphlets to gain knowledge and insight as to what you are being faced with. As to the issues and whether or not these things should be done? My thoughts and wishes don't weigh here at all, honey, nor should they. I won't say what I think. If you want clinical or medical answers, I will help with what I can, but don't ask me for my opinion on what to do—it's not my place. Gaye's husband and children should make these decisions, not me. I love Gaye in my own way, and I want what's best for her. But I am not the decision maker here. I'm sorry, but it is up to you and the kids," I explained to him as gently as I could.

It was then that he lost it. He couldn't contain his emotions any longer. He sobbed in my arms, saying, "She never deserved this. This is so unfair!" Holding him there, I sobbed as well. I sobbed for Gaye, Eric, the kids and for me. The love of my life's heart was breaking—how could I not be affected? As he gathered himself, he began to peruse the pamphlets. Tears, again, welled up in his eyes as he tried to understand what he was reading.

"You seem to have read the pamphlets a half dozen times," I finally said to him.

"I know," he replied in a sad voice, "my mind seems to be somewhere else."

"Here, let me read them to you and we can discuss what we've read. That way you'll better understand what's written," I offered.

"Good idea," he said as he held me tight.

I read the pamphlets and went over the information with him a little at a time. He had few questions, and by the time we had finished, he seemed to have gathered his thoughts. "I think I'll call Mel first," he said. "She'll help me decide who should talk to Rix."

Eric loved his son dearly, but he was worried that perhaps he wouldn't be able to broach the subject with him in a gentle enough manner. He'd leave it up to Mel as to who should tell him. I poured Eric a diet Coke, sat it down on the table beside him and proceeded to leave the room.

"Where are you going, hon?" Eric asked me.

"I'll wait in the bedroom while you talk to your children. This is not a place for me, and you need to be free to discuss whatever it is you have to without me in the room," I explained.

"But I think it would help me to have you here," he pleaded as he got up to meet me and take my hand.

"There's nothing I can do for you while you're discussing this with the kids. Just know I'll be in the next room if you need me. This really is a time when it needs to be you and the kids," I tried to convince him.

"OK, I don't agree, but OK," he said as he kissed my forehead. I gave him a little hug and left the room. I retreated to our room, shut the door and turned on the TV to keep me company. Although I truly believed that I had made the right decision to leave him alone with his kids, I felt so isolated sitting in our room watching TV. I was sure this wasn't the only time I would feel alone where Gaye was concerned, but it wasn't about me. It was about what they needed to do as a family.

After the phone call, Eric explained to me that, for her, Mel felt that nothing should be done to prolong her mom's illness. She was ready for her mother to be free of the body that imprisoned her. Mel told her dad she would call Rix and ask what he thought and would call him back as soon as they spoke.

Once Mel had her conversation with Rix, he told her he wanted to discuss it with Emily and would let her know. A few days later, Mel called us and informed us that Rix agreed with Mel and Eric. No feeding tube and no IV hydration.

Eric went down to the nursing home the next day and signed the paperwork; it was now in writing as well as understood. They all wanted Gaye's nightmare to be over, for her to be whole again and to be able to relive the memories she had created over her fifty-plus years. Everyone in the family believed that a better life awaited Gaye, a life in which her memories would be restored intact.

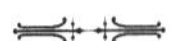

CHAPTER 14
CONTINUED PAIN

Eric and I cherished our time with each other and wished we could be together 24/7. We always have felt like we are making up for lost time, so when it was my turn to work weekends or holidays at the hospital, we would dread it. I had moved back up to the pediatric floor because I missed being with my young patients. Children gave me energy; I needed to be with them and felt that they needed me. I loved the ER and what I had learned there, but the gift I have with children put me right back where I belonged, taking care of them.

Ten months after I went back to the pediatric floor, Eric found an ad in the local newspaper for an RN. It was for a pediatric office in Monument, about ten minutes from our home. "Hon, look. There's a job in Monument for an RN. It's at a pediatric office, just your specialty!" he exclaimed.

"Eric, a doctor's office wouldn't pay me nearly what I make at the hospital," I told him.

"Yes, but you'd have weekends and holidays off. Just what we want! At least look into it," he pleaded.

After a lot of soul searching, I thought I'd at least check it out. After a few emails and spontaneous interviews (one done on the phone in my car), they offered me a job and I called Eric to tell him. "So when do you start?" he asked me.

"I haven't taken the job yet," I told him.

"Why not?" he asked.

"It's a huge pay cut. Almost nine dollars an hour! I can't afford to take that kind of a cut," I explained.

"I can help you out," he said. "My retirement checks along with my new job will be plenty for us to live on." (Eric had recently retired after thirty-seven years civil service for the military and would be drawing retirement pay as well as working as a contractor for one of the air force bases in town.)

"I can take care of the bills you can't afford anymore," he explained. "Do you think you'd like the job? That's more important than anything," he added.

"Eric, it doesn't matter where I go to take care of children; as long as I am taking care of them, I'll be happy. I know I'll miss hospital nursing, but I'll be with children and that's all that matters!" I told him, as I began to feel excited about having the weekends off.

I took the job and started November 9. That Thanksgiving I was getting paid while making Thanksgiving dinner—who would have thought! I loved my new job, the providers and the staff. We would have our issues figuring out how I fit into the puzzle. But eventually, it would all work out and be one of the most rewarding jobs I have ever had. And I was right—it didn't matter where I was, as long as I was taking care of children. I was happy...very happy!

Although life seemed to be going as it should, we all still had to deal with the impending loss of Gaye. I tried to be sympathetic to everyone's needs and tried to understand them for myself as well as for them. It was at about this time when I began to notice a change in Brian, Eric's youngest grandchild. Children have always taken to me. They can sense that I am trustworthy and know I would never do anything to harm them. I can, and have, dealt with a child that wasn't quite three years old and talked her through letting me draw blood from her arm; and she held still. Children just trust me and like me immediately. Brian was no different. He once told me that he would protect me from the headless horsemen while we were watching a play his sister was in. I never questioned that he cared for me.

But during the fall of 2009, he began to change toward me. When we saw him, he wouldn't run up and hug me as was his usual way of greeting me. Instead, I would go to hug him, only to find his arms straight down his sides as though he were merely being polite in letting me hug him. I would rather a child not like me than be polite to me in this way. I expressed my concern to Eric. He, being a man, thought I was overanalyzing and dismissed the whole thing. By that following Christmas, we would have a bit more insight into to what was going on.

Of course, we were planning a big family Christmas in our new home. We were so excited, until the day we got an email from Rix. He explained that Megan wouldn't be coming to Christmas this year. She felt that what her Grandpa was doing was wrong. Marriage, she believed, was until "death do us part," and her Grandma wasn't gone and she didn't approve. Rix explained in the letter that they had raised her with good Christian values and she was just expressing her opinion. I was crushed.

I didn't expect Megan to change her mind, nor would I even try to change her mind about our situation and how she needed to deal with it. But now I understood why Brian was acting the way he was. Eric and I were sure Megan might have been in conversation with him about "things," which would explain his behavior. As sad as it was, the truth is that Brian didn't remember his grandmother. He was a toddler when she went into the nursing home. It was obvious that the loss of Gaye was extremely upsetting to Megan. She needed to voice her opinion in support and protection of her grandmother, since she couldn't speak for herself.

At this point, I wished that Megan knew of my love for Gaye and my visits with her; but I never spoke of this with her. Perhaps I should have. But at the time, I believed that what I shared with Gaye, was truly between her and me, and I only confided with Eric. As hurtful as it all was, I understood that Megan felt she was doing what was right. It was her way of dealing with this unfair situation in which she was caught up.

Eric promptly sent Rix a reply about how he felt. He explained that he had spent a long time figuring out what he should do, and what Gaye would want him to do, before he even considered dating anyone. Eric also reminded Rix that it was Mel who had actually talked him into dating, with the whole family behind her. He got a short reply from Rix, telling him that he and his wife didn't have a problem with the situation, that he was just explaining Megan's feelings. Rix also agreed that he supported his dad in moving on and finding happiness, and that he was glad that his father now had what he needed.

It was at this time that I decided to send an email to Rix myself. It was a heartfelt email giving my perspective on his dad's situation. My hope was to shed light on it in a way that might help him explain the situation to his daughter:

Rix,

Please read this in its entirety...It's from me, Tami. I prayed for strength and the right words before I started...

I've had to sit back and watch the deterioration of a relationship all over a child's misconception of the world around her. I'm done hurting and need it to stop for me. I feel I need to say what I need to say. Perhaps if you share this letter with Megan, she might gain some insight...She might not, but it's worth a chance.

When we met, your dad spared no time in telling me about your mom and his situation. I believe he told me in the first twenty minutes of our first conversation. The next few days were a whirlwind of emotions, but, unfortunately, I didn't spend any time thinking about the situation. I was caught up in strong feelings for a man whom I felt, yes even from the very beginning, I belonged with. If I had spent any time in thought about where I was putting myself, things might have turned out differently. In the position of the "other woman" is not where I had ever pictured myself.

You see, things are not always as they appear. It seems that there are those who think that the journey your dad and I are taking is so very easy. That people are forgotten and life moved on without them is a misconception. On the contrary, I am reminded daily that I am, legally, not your father's wife. We are not allowed the luxuries of being legally married. We are not allowed to "move on" completely. And now, we are not even allowed, by certain family members, to enjoy what we do have and are being made to feel that what we are doing, we should be ashamed of.

I was brought up in a conservative Christian family. I raised my children in a conservative Christian family. But in addition, I, being raised in a deaf home, learned quickly of the differences in people...so therefore, I became accepting of anyone and/or any situation. Because my kids were raised with not only deaf grandparents, but also severely disabled family members, as well as gay members, they, too, grew up with the value of people and the value of acceptance, and they know that it is not their place to judge. I feel that His plan is that we are to learn while we are here and I feel the most important part of what we are to learn is to love. I feel it is what the whole New Testament is about: the love Jesus had for everyone, regardless of their choices or who they were. If someone is to live by the Bible, it needs to be by the whole Bible, not just the parts they want to pick and choose.

Has Megan read the New Testament? The stories of love and acceptance that Jesus teaches us might give her some new insight into what life is supposed to be about. I believe that the talks Emily is having with Megan are a great start. But one has to choose the right words, and more importantly, one has to set the right examples. True acceptance is spoken without words. Maybe you could remind her that the marriage phrase "in sickness and in health, till death do us part" is not from the Bible but from the Book of Common Prayer. I am not defending what we're doing based on this because I do believe in these words. But they were not the words of God, but of Man. Matthew 22:29: Jesus replied, "You are in error because you do not know the scriptures or the power of God." Your dad took great pains and efforts to take care of your mom in sickness...to the point of his own health deteriorating. There had to be an end to it.

There is a side of the situation that no one bothers to think about. I fell in love with a man who is still in love with his first wife. Can you imagine how difficult that is in itself? We are not free to marry. We are not free to have the law see us as married. We can't even be on the same insurance policy together, yet we are married in every sense of the word. The emotions I face daily, no one can guess. But yet, I choose to be here.

I chose to have your mother's pictures in the other house. It was I who put those pictures out. No one is being forgotten. Like your dad told you in a previous letter, we are putting together a wall of family pictures...I planned on your mom being there too; it is because of her that there is a family for me to love, so I want her there. This is difficult for me and then it's not. I, from the beginning, never wanted anyone to think that your mom is forgotten. I never wanted anyone to think that I wanted to replace her. Rix, I love your mother. I never knew her, but I love her because she gave me wonderful children and beautiful grandchildren to love, because her family wouldn't be so wonderful if she wasn't a wonderful person too. I love her because your father loves her. I love her because I am sorry for her pain but mostly because she is a child of God.

My friends don't know where I get the strength to deal with this situation as I have. I'm not sure whether you know this about me or not, but I am not a "strong" person by nature. But I have an inner strength to help heal your father as well as the rest of this family, if they'll let me...The strength comes from God...I know that just as sure as I am sitting here. Your dad and I both believe that it was He who brought us together. That it was He who knew the kind of woman it would take to be put in this very difficult situation, one with endless love and acceptance. He knew what kind of love we could bring to each other as well as to the rest of the family to help promote healing from the nightmare. I embraced his children and loved them as my own, knowing full well, and rightfully so, that I was not a replacement nor would I ever try to replace their dear mother.

I love you guys because you are your father's children, I love you guys because of the wonderful people you are, I love you because you love your mother, I love you because you are your mother and your father, and I love you because of the wonderful families you are raising. I love you guys because your mother can't be here to do it. I embraced your father's grandchildren because they are all wonderful, because they are all his grandchildren, because they all have their own conscience and are true to their beliefs, because they are all beautiful spirits, and because their grandmother can't be here for them anymore.

So, you see, we feel that we are being guided by Him. So if we are being guided by Him, how can any of this be wrong?? I don't pretend to understand why it is this way. Why your mother still lingers in her silent world. Why your dad and I didn't meet when this was all over. I don't understand it any more than you do, but it is what is given to us. I pray 3–4 times a day. I am in constant conversation with Him. He has been my strength my entire life, my inner light that everyone calls my "glow." I know why I'm here; I know my duties and what is expected of me. But most of all, I never make a decision without discussing it with Him...and it was He who led me to write this letter. How could anything guided by Him be wrong??

I love you.

Tami:)

I sent the email but, after many discussions, Eric and I realized that whatever Megan's opinions were, she had the right to how she felt, and we would respect her love and devotion for her grandmother.

We also realized that she was young and unable to assess the situation completely, but her strength to stand by her feelings was admirable.

To say the least, the emails caused me deep pain. I did understand Megan's feelings but was deeply hurt, because I felt that she would never accept me for who I was to the family, her grandpa or even to her grandmother. Megan had no idea of the role I was playing in this nightmare. I hoped that someday she would see that I was just as much here for her grandmother as I was for anyone, that I felt a love for someone I'd never met before her illness. And I wished she could know that my love for Gaye was as powerful and deep as it would have been if I had known her all my life. Christmas just didn't seem to be Christmas after the emails. But I tried as best I could to bring the spirit into our home, in spite of it all.

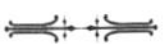

Typically Christmas was spent with Eric's children and grandchildren on Christmas Eve, because Emily and Rix liked to reserve waking up Christmas morning at home for little Brian, and then spending the day with her parents. This usually meant that Jamie, Mel's husband who was in retail, was never at the family Christmas gatherings. In light of the situation, Eric made the decision that Christmas, this year, would be celebrated at our house on Christmas Day, so that Jamie could attend. But of course, that meant that Rix's family wouldn't be coming. I was glad that Jamie would finally be with us but heartbroken that Rix's family wouldn't be there at all. Mel was thrilled, to say the least, that we were having the festivities on Christmas Day so Jamie could be there.

"Finally!" she told her dad over the phone when he explained the plan for that Christmas. "Finally, Jamie gets to come! I'm so excited! Shame on Megan for not understanding or accepting the decisions you are making in your life. Shame on her. But yay for us. We get to have Christmas with Jamie!"

Christmas was very nice. My three kids were present as well as Mel's family. But it felt odd and I was hurting. The hurt that I felt was as though I were the cause of Rix not coming. If it weren't for me, Rix and his family would be here with Eric for Christmas. I was uncomfortable because some of the people who meant the most to me didn't approve of me and the situation.

At one point during the festivities, Mel could sense that I was down. She took me aside and tried to make me feel better. "You have to know, this is all wrong. I can't imagine that Megan would ever have made any preconceived judgments on this situation. I am sure someone has her convinced that what you and Dad share is all wrong."

Whoever it was, it didn't matter to me. At least one of them didn't approve, and it hurt. "Mel, it could be Megan," I told her, choosing not to believe that anyone else would purposely try to drive a wedge between the families. "Megan may be protecting her grandmother or even just dealing with this nightmare in her own way. For whatever reason, it doesn't matter. I am going to feel responsible because I am here, and they are not," I told her. "It's Christmas and you should all be together."

"We are all together," Mel assured me. "We are all together celebrating with love. I am sorry they are missing out, but it was their choice. If my boys were to voice an opinion like Megan did, I would explain the situation to them completely. I would explain it in a way where they could see all sides of what was going on. The difference between my boys and Rix's kids is that my boys witnessed the depressed man my dad used to be; they know, firsthand, how miserable he was and now they see how happy he is. They know it's because of you. They feel like you love them and are here for them as well as for me. And they know how much you continue to make my mom a part of all of our lives. They know what you are to this family; I am sorry for Megan or anyone else who doesn't see that. Megan hasn't been around my father like we have; she doesn't know the pain he's had to endure, like we have. They are missing out on the joy that you have brought to Dad and to our family, and I feel sorry for theirs!"

Her words lifted my spirits enough that I realized it was Christmas and I wasn't going to let anything or anyone bring me down. The rest of the day was truly joyful. We were a family moving forward as best we could in the situation we were in, and we took joy in being together.

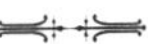

Eric wanted to take Rix's family their gifts the following day. I supported his actions completely. He needed to connect with his son and family to let them know he loved them and wished them happiness as always. It was while Eric was getting ready to go that he noticed I wasn't making my own preparations. When he asked why, I explained, "I can't go with you. I would be subjecting myself to even more pain than I have already endured and making everyone uncomfortable, especially Megan. You go, give them the gifts and my love and have a wonderful visit," I told him, trying to fight back tears.

He wasn't having it. He wanted me with him, saying that if I didn't go, he would be hurt. I was firm in my decision and told him that it was hurtful either way and no one wins, that he needed to do what he must, and I needed to protect myself and respect Megan's feelings as well.

When he left the house, all I could do was cry. I hurt for myself but also for the family—for anyone and everyone in the family who might have ideas that Eric was not acting appropriately. I knew how Mel and Rix felt about their dad finding happiness. I knew that even Ila, Gaye's mother, approved and couldn't be happier for Eric and me. My children had, on several occasions, voiced their opinions about my role in Eric's family; they knew my heart and my intentions. They knew me better than anyone and recognized that I would give until there was nothing left to give, even to those family members who didn't approve.

My concerns were for family members who were affected like Megan, but who chose to remain silent. Who else, besides the immediate family, felt that what Eric was doing was wrong? It was one of the first times I actually felt shame and needed to talk to someone. But I soon realized that I had put myself in this situation, and I wouldn't burden anyone with my sorrow, especially around the holidays. Eric knew I was hurting, which prompted him to call and check on me several times on his way to Longmont.

"Hon, you sound so down," he said on one of the phone calls.

"Well, I am, I guess, but I'll be fine. Give them all my love, OK?" I said.

"Of course I will. I wish you were here with me, though," he said.

When he arrived home, I was my usual happy self. I had caused Eric enough grief over this entire situation; I wanted it to be done. He gave me Christmas gifts that he said Rix had picked out himself.

I know, deep down, that Rix has a place for me in his heart. It is not the place that his mother occupies, nor would I ever assume to be anywhere near that special place. But it is a place for the woman who brought his father back to life and back into the grandchildren's lives, and who was helping him through the toughest time of his life. I could be wrong in my feelings of his sentiment toward me, but his actions have always made me feel this way.

The gifts were very thoughtful and I appreciated them and called with a heartfelt thanks to him and Emily. When Brian came on the phone to thank me for his gift, I had to hand the phone to Eric. My heart hurt that I had missed Christmas with him.

After the phone call, Eric explained that as he neared Rix's home he called to let him know he was approaching. Rix then asked his father what we wanted to do about lunch. Eric explained to his son that I wasn't with him. Eric also told me that he could hear disbelief in his son's voice that I wasn't with him. When Eric told me of this, I wondered what they had expected? It was clear that Megan didn't approve and didn't want to be around me, so why would I go and make her feel uncomfortable in her own home?

In such an atmosphere of tension, Christmas finally came to an end. It was the first time in my life that I had ever felt like I couldn't wait for it to be over.

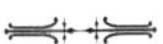

Don, Eric's brother, up to this point had never really spoken of Gaye to me. I can't recall him even mentioning her name. I have realized that perhaps he is a man of few words, when it comes to his feelings. Maybe not mentioning Gaye helps him deal with the loss.

Because of the close relationship between Gaye and Don's wife, Madlyn, I felt at a disadvantage, coming in at such a late stage in the game. That, coupled with the fact that Don and Madlyn moved to Arizona soon after I met Eric, didn't help her and me develop any kind of a relationship. I know she has supported Eric in his decisions regarding our relationship. She is a sweet, caring human being and wants what's best for her brother-in-law. But somehow, to this day, I have always felt that Madlyn didn't approve of me for Eric. Her comment that I was a "spring chicken" had initially signaled disapproval to me. And later I found out that Madlyn had told the family, even extended family members, every detail she knew about me, before I had ever met them. I don't really know the motivation behind her actions but what I do know, now, is that Madlyn's heart is pure in its intentions. There was no intended maliciousness in any of her actions or words. And any reservations she may have had towards me, was based purely on her love and devotion for Eric and Gaye.

But it did seem that there was a wall between us. I concluded that Madlyn was protecting her relationship with Gaye, and that she missed her sister-in-law dearly, mourned her illness and felt pain for her own loss. Madlyn, I decided, was yet another victim of Alzheimer's—along with the rest of the family. She and every other family member had to cope with their grief, each in their own way.

⁂

The first time I met Donnie, Gaye's sister, I was afraid it would be uncomfortable. But she was warm, welcoming and glad to meet the woman who was making Eric happy. The morning after we arrived at her home, she and I had a long conversation. She thought it was wonderful that Eric was finally able to move on, and she was pleased to have me in the family. She also told me she hadn't seen Eric this happy in years. I never felt more a part of this family as I did when I talked to her.

I knew she was genuine and wanted what was best for Eric, but I could see her pain. Several times during our conversation that morning, she broke down in tears. She missed her sister terribly and ached for the thought of her living her young life locked away in a nursing home. She took me by the hand and led me into her kitchen and motioned for me to look at the wall above her sink. There, displayed proudly, was the rolling pin that Eric and I had sent her the Christmas before. It was a rolling pin on which Gaye had beautifully painted a scene of a country kitchen shelf. "I look at it every day," she told me. "It helps me remember the sister that I had before the disease and to think positively about where she'll be when it's all over. That's the Gaye I want to remember," she said as we embraced and cried together.

"That's the Gaye she wants you to remember," I whispered to her.

Ila and I have had a couple of long discussions. While Ila has never really confided in me about her feelings about her daughter and her illness, she did tell me this: No mother ever wants to bury her own child. Being a pediatric nurse and mother, I understood this, probably more than most, and more than I wished I ever had to. She also said that, no matter the age of the child, it cuts like a knife to lose one. On more than one occasion, Ila made it clear to me that she was happy that I was in the family and "taking care of things" for Eric and the rest of the family. I remember thinking once, after leaving her home in Idaho Falls, that her strength must come from having suffered through the illness of her own mother and from the conviction that Gaye would someday be free of her disease.

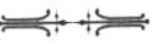

Right before I was to meet Eric's parents for the first time, Melanie and Rix filled me in on their thoughts of their grandparents. What I gathered from the conversations was that their grandparents were conservative in their views and held fast to them. With this in mind, I was scared to death to meet them. First of all, would Eric's mother also think I was too young for him? And secondly, did they approve of their son "carrying on" with another woman while his wife was still living? Eric is not real close to his parents, so I really couldn't rely on any insight from him as to how they'd accept me. He did once tell me that if I invited them to dinner, they might decline. This sent a streak of horror down into the depths of my soul. I know that it didn't matter to Eric what his parents thought of our situation, but it mattered to me.

On our first meeting, I found them to be pleasant and extremely accepting of me and our situation. They genuinely seemed happy for Eric. They, too, had their own difficulties in dealing with Gaye's illness. According to Eric, during the first year that Gaye was moved to the nursing home, his parents were visiting Colorado Springs (from Florida where they lived at the time) and declined to visit Gaye. Eric explained to me that he was offended by his parents lack of caring, as he saw it. I tried to get him to see that, perhaps, it was just their way of coping. Maybe it would be too painful for them to see her in a nursing home, so he shouldn't be too harsh on them. I pointed out that they continued to remember Gaye every Christmas and on her birthday with a gift that we would take to her in the nursing home. And they even remembered her on Eric and Gaye's anniversary with a card and a gift. I tried to get him to see that they had not forgotten Gaye; it was just how they dealt with the situation. Eric seemed to accept my possible explanation of their actions, but I could see that he was still hurt.

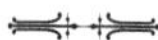

Gaye continued to hold on to life, yet she was missed by everyone she loved, and who loved her, as if she were gone. This is one of the tragedies of Alzheimer's: No one is allowed to have closure until the disease deems it to be time. The pain that the family all endured was compounded by the thought that Gaye was not gone, but wasting away in the nursing home. Everyone has had to deal with feelings of loss individually, and no one should judge what is right and what is wrong. As for me, I felt I was brought to the family to help in any way I could. I saw it as my role to bring peace and love to them during their time of mourning and loss. I wanted to be there not just for Eric, but for everyone and anyone who needed my support. What I didn't really take into account was how difficult it was all going to be.

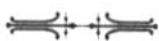

CHAPTER 15

THE BEGINNING OF THE END

My birthday is in January, not too long after Christmas. Much to my delight, Rix sent me flowers. In the past, he had never really acknowledged my birthday; not many in my "new family" even know when my birthday is, so it was a beautiful surprise! I wondered if the flowers were a sort of peace offering after what had happened at Christmas. I wondered if perhaps Rix realized that I was hurt and so sent the flowers. No matter what his intentions, I thought it was a beautiful gesture and embraced it wholeheartedly. I knew that no one had intended to cause me pain and, as far as I was concerned, the whole sadness was put away with the last Christmas decoration.

In March, we got a phone call from the nursing home. "Gaye has pneumonia. Do you want us to give her antibiotics?" was the question the nursing home staff asked Eric. Eric looked to me, again, for an answer. I told him, again, it was a decision for him and the kids. Eric called Melanie, who was flatly against it. "Why would I want to prolong her life the way it is?" she asked her father. She then told him that she would call and ask Rix and call him back when she had his answer.

A couple of days later she called and informed her dad that she was in shock, as Rix wanted Gaye to have antibiotics. He felt it wasn't much different than giving her vitamins. Mel felt that it was now entirely Eric's decision, since she and Rix were split on the issue at hand. Eric, after speaking with the nursing home staff about the antibiotics, decided that there would be none. He knew in his heart of hearts that his wife would not want to prolong her confinement. He informed the nursing home and, again, papers were signed.

Gaye recovered from whatever illness she had, without antibiotics. Eric was somewhat glad about the incident, which he described as preparation for "times to come." He believed that the document needed to be in place, because if he were faced with an emergency situation, he was afraid he wouldn't be able to think logically enough to make the best decision. Over the past two years, we had been on a roller coaster when it came to Gaye's health. Her rapid weight loss had a few times brought the family hope that she would soon be free from her body. But her body held on, her young heart kept beating and we lived day to day.

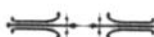

Then, on Friday, April 16, 2010, Eric and I had the day off to attend a couple of his appointments and run errands. In between appointments, Melanie called. "Hospice says Mom has pneumonia and won't make it through the weekend."

Eric and I rushed to the nursing home. When we got down there, I did a quick assessment. I didn't feel she looked as close to death as the hospice staff had indicated, but I was no expert in these matters. I called Melanie and told her my findings. "She's not mottled, her breathing isn't labored. Her cap refill is slow, about five to seven seconds, and her pedal pulses are weak but palpable. Mel, since you have your care plans today for clinical in the morning, I don't think you need to come now."

She was thankful I was there to inform her of my findings and agreed to stay home. Nursing school was grueling enough without having to deal with such an abominable situation. Eric and I headed back to our house. Soon after arriving home, we got a phone call from Rix.

"You're where?" Eric said. "On Baptist Road? Yes we're home. See you in a bit."

Mel had called Rix and informed him of that the hospice staff thought that his mother wouldn't last the weekend. Rix left work and, as soon as he could, headed to the Springs to be with his mother. He was already on the way when Mel called him to tell him what I had told her. He decided that since he was almost here, he would come anyway and stay the night if necessary. It was at that point that Mel decided to come up from Pueblo. In spite of her studies, she needed to be with her family at this time.

Rix arrived shortly and I fixed him a sandwich. He and Eric got ready to leave for the nursing home. I felt that this was not a time for me to be around. The family needed to be with Gaye; it was their moment to be with each other and for each other. This was private time that they needed to share, without an outsider.

I told Eric I would be staying home. "But I want and need you there," Eric pleaded.

"I know you do. But your family will be there for you. Really, Eric, let them be there for you. This is your time with your family. However sad it is, embrace it and be there for them as well."

He finally dropped the subject, and he and Rix headed out. I busied myself with chores to keep my mind occupied, but my heart and thoughts were heavy with the pain that the family was facing.

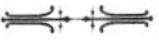

Not being at the nursing home, I had no idea what transpired. Melanie, Rix and Eric filled me in on the details of the visit.

During the time that I was writing this book, Rix informed me that he was nervous about seeing his mom so close to death. The only "death experience" that he'd had was when his wife's grandfather had passed away, and that had just involved his attending the funeral. "We, Melanie and I, have already grieved our mom's illness and her 'passing.' She wasn't our mom anymore and we each said our goodbyes a long time before she actually passed away," he told me. So, for Gaye's children, it wasn't about grief at that point, but about "taking care of what needed to be done."

Eric and Rix arrived and waited for Melanie in the "living room" of the nursing home. As she walked in, they stood up from the couch they were sitting on and greeted each other with a hug and solemn faces. They walked into Gaye's room to see her lying in the bed with oxygen, but resting comfortably. There were nurses, assistants and the hospice nurse in her room. The staff were all telling Gaye that they loved her and that she would be missed. Rix, Eric and Mel were moved at all the love and care that they had for Gaye. Eric went to Gaye's bedside and took her contractured hands into his and, through tears and a shaking voice, told her he loved her. He kissed her on her forehead, stood up and hugged Mel. It was a difficult and painful situation that they wanted an end to, but the grief was still there.

At the hospice nurse's urging, the family decided they should go to the funeral home to "make arrangements" for when Gaye would pass. Since there were no signs that Gaye would be passing immediately, they decided to take the nurse's advice.

Once at the funeral home, they waited for the director to join them. There was a small gathering for an employee that afternoon, and things seemed disorganized. Eric was his usual impatient self. Rix and Mel tried to make light of the situation and joked a bit to ease the mood. Eric wanted to leave, but Melanie, true to form in wanting to get things done, put her foot down. "Under no circumstances are we leaving, Dad. We need to take care of this and we're going to do it now. We have no idea when Mom is going to pass away, so we need to get prepared for when it happens," she said.

Finally, a director joined them, apologized for the tardiness and helped them make the decisions that no one wants to make for a loved one. Small urns were selected for family members who would want them, but the rest of Gaye's remains would go into a vase that she made when she was a girl in high school. Mel talked to the funeral director about using the vase; he assured her that it was fine and that he would seal it appropriately for burial.

On their way to the funeral home Eric had called me. "We're going to make the final arrangements; then I'll call you and we'll all meet for dinner."

"Final arrangements"—those words hit me like a brick. I guessed that they felt it was necessary. I began to weep. I felt both happy and sad tears—happy for the end of Gaye's suffering but sad because the family will have to finally say good-bye to their beloved Gaye. The pain that would be endured by everyone would be welcomed as an end, but an arduous one, nonetheless. I felt isolated and helpless, but I was extremely grateful that Eric had his children with him, supporting him and helping him make some extremely difficult decisions at the funeral home. Little did I know that my feelings were just touching on a myriad of emotions to come. Over the next week, there would be many more emotions that I and everyone else would have to brave.

When we met for dinner, we decided that Rix would stay over with us on the chance that something might happen during the night. But by the next morning, it was evident that Gaye would make it through the weekend. When it became clear that there was no change in her condition, Rix went home. To help ease Mel's mind about going back to Pueblo, I told her that I would visit Gaye every day to keep her posted. She was appreciative and said she would be anxiously awaiting my calls.

That evening, I sat next to Eric on the couch and looked him in the eyes.

"I need you to promise me something. I need you to *feel* everything. Don't skip over anything or any feeling because it's too difficult or hurts too much. To truly heal from this, you need to feel it all. Gaye was your wife, the mother of your children, the love of your life. You need to mourn her passing. You need to feel everything that goes along with that, no matter who is around."

He looked back at me with those sad, soulful eyes that I hadn't seen since our first meeting and said, through tears, "I promise."

That following Sunday, not only was Gaye still here but she had eaten 75 percent of her afternoon meal. I called Mel from her mother's bedside at the nursing home.

"Your mom is eating again and she's off the oxygen. Her condition has actually improved," I reported.

Mel had a "meltdown." "I don't want her to start eating again!" she cried when I called her with the news. "I don't want her to get better! I need her to go! I can't do this constant roller coaster anymore. I needed this to be done! I love my mother, but I need this to be over for both of us!" She began to sob.

"I know, I know, I understand," I reassured her. "Look, Mel, I'll come check on her tomorrow and call you then. Sometimes there is a sort of 'rebound' of one's health before death. I'll call you again tomorrow. Try to get some rest." My attempt to comfort her seemed to have helped. She calmed down and we hung up the phone.

I knew what she was saying. It wasn't that she didn't love her mother. She loved her dearly, but she was tired. She was tired for her mom and for herself.

When I came home, I told Eric of the conversation with Melanie. He looked at me and seemed to agree but didn't verbalize it. The look on his face told me he wanted Gaye to be at peace. But Eric, being the man he is, would feel that to articulate such a statement might be thought of as betrayal, so he kept silent.

Monday, after work and dinner, I went to the nursing home. I called Mel to give her my report. "The CNA said she is refusing her protein shakes but is drinking her juices and not running fevers anymore. Her eyes seem a bit more sunken, but everything else is the same," I reported.

When I returned home, Eric seemed to be in a strange place. He finally looked at me and said, with tears streaming down his face, "I agree with Mel—it's time for her to go. It's time to put an end to all this for everyone, especially for her."

The following day I had little to no energy. I was physically exhausted from all the emotional stress. I left work for my lunch hour a bit early to go to the nursing home. Gaye's eyes were even more sunken, so much so that her eyebrows were no longer on her brow bone; she looked emaciated. I called Melanie with my daily report.

"She's still drinking juices, not on oxygen, no fever. She does look a bit more emaciated today, though. But otherwise she seems the same," I told Mel.

I also told her I wouldn't be going down again the following day. I needed a break and thought that Gaye would not possibly change dramatically in the next twenty-four hours. Mel understood.

On Thursday night, when I arrived at the nursing home, I noticed that there had been a huge change since the day before yesterday. Gaye's whole face was extremely emaciated. Her CNA said she was now refusing everything, even juice.

I called Mel and gave her the news. "She also has a bounding pulse and is on three liters of oxygen. Mel, she doesn't even seem like the same person I saw two days ago."

She hesitated then said, "I don't have care plans this weekend and no tests to study for, so I am going to come down tomorrow."

Eric took Friday off, knowing that Melanie would be at the nursing home and feeling like he needed to be available. He informed me that he needed to drop off the insurance card and finish discussions with the funeral director; then he would meet Mel at the nursing home.

I, too, was off that day and said, "Call me when you're done; I'll be in town myself because I have some things to take care of with Amanda."

He kissed me good-bye and headed out. On my way into town, I prayed for the family; I prayed that their pain would soon be over.

During lunch that day with Amanda and her father, I got a phone call from Eric; he could barely speak through his tears. "Mel is at the nursing home; she called me while I was down at the funeral home. Gaye is much worse."

"OK, I'll meet you down there," I said. I noticed that Amanda was in tears. "I would like to go with you, Mom."

"No I don't think this is the time, but I will tell Eric you wanted to be there," I said, trying to comfort her.

Tim looked puzzled and asked our daughter, "Are you OK, Amanda?"

I put my arm around her, looked at him and said, "She's just hurting for Eric."

She nodded in confirmation of my guess. She loves Eric and cares for him very much; it was so very evident at that moment that she felt his pain.

I headed to the nursing home, knowing that what was to come would be tough.

Mel was in tears sitting by her mom's bedside. "I know you tried to prepare me, but I lost it when I got here because I couldn't believe what she looked like," she said. "She's now on five liters of oxygen and they won't give her any more. She's getting Roxinol (liquid morphine), scheduled around the clock and she's also getting fever control. They said she was having infectious sputum. I really think this might be it."

Her tears seemed to abate as we talked a bit about Eric. "Your dad should be here any minute; he was leaving the funeral home when I spoke to him," I told her.

A few minutes later Eric walked in, his face in pain as tears welled up in his eyes. As he came towards me, I moved out of the way a bit so he would hug Melanie first. This was their family hurting and, once again, I didn't want to be an intruder. I was there to help, but not to intrude.

They clung to each other and I stood there holding myself, feeling their sorrow. It was a priceless gift to watch them embrace and share their pain in that intimate moment. It was hard to see them both in such pain but beautiful that their relationship was such that they could hold each other up during this saddest of moments. But at the same time I had to emotionally leave. I had always known that the closer we got to Gaye's passing, the more difficult my emotions would be to manage, but I had to be strong. In all honesty, though, tears burned my eyes and my heart ached.

After what seemed like forever, Mel told Eric what was going on. Mel and I stepped out of the room to leave Eric with his beloved.

Once we were in the hallway, she said, "My dad would never get through this without you. Before he met you, I really think he was on a mission to die. His reckless behavior, drinking, motorcycle riding without a helmet and smoking had me convinced he would have died without you. Thank you."

I knew Mel felt this way, as she had told me this so many times over the past two years, but it was nice to hear again.

Eric came out of the room and we all went back in. We sat there a while then I excused myself to go to the bathroom and to talk to Gaye's nurse about the doses of her medications.

I couldn't fight the feelings anymore. I hurried to the restroom, closed the door behind me, sat in a heap on the floor and cried. I had to get all my own tears out of me before I faced anyone again. After a few minutes, I gathered my strength and approached the nurses' station.

I came back and told them what I had learned about the dosage; it would keep Gaye as comfortable as possible. We all agreed that she looked as though she was not in pain and that she was resting peacefully.

After a while, Eric said, "OK, Mel, I want you to go home and be with your family."

She looked up at him and said, "Really?" with a look of disbelief that her dad had made such a decision so abruptly.

He nodded and she said, "OK, but I need to tell mom some things first."

Eric and I left the room and walked down the hall to make sure that they knew to call him first if anything happened. While we were at the nurses' station, a nurse came up to Eric and said, "Your daughter needs you, now." He went back in the room, I heard Mel talking through tears, but I couldn't understand her words. After a few moments, they emerged from her room. I put my arm around Mel as we walked down the hall. "You OK?" I asked.

She nodded her head yes and said, "I was telling my mom some things about the boys, how she would be proud of them, that I was going to nursing school and that she needed to go and be free of her body. Then I saw that a tear ran down out of her left eye and that she had one in the corner of her right eye. I know she heard me!"

I was both horrified and joyous at this news. Joyous because Mel must have felt a moment of connection with her mom, but horrified at thinking that perhaps she's been "in there" all along, feeling every contracture, knowing what she was being reduced to...I tried to put it out of my mind; it was too painful and frightening to visit. As we left the nursing home, we said our good-byes and Eric assured Mel that he would visit Gaye that evening and give her a report. I went to pick up Amanda and met up with Eric at home.

After dinner, when Amanda had gone to the neighbor's to babysit, Eric said, "I want to go to the nursing home and stay the night with Gaye."

I understood. He didn't want Gaye to be alone when she passed away, and neither did I. He left around 9:30. I closed the door of the garage behind him and sank to the floor in tears. I felt his pain, admired his love and loyalty to Gaye, and revisited the fact that she was "the love of his life"; I knew that he loved me, but I was not Gaye.

I hurt so much; I went to bed and tried to pull myself out of self-pity. Remembering the admiration I had for his devotion to his wife helped, as it was one of the reasons I loved him so much. But at this moment, I felt as though I were the "other woman." My bed was abandoned for hers. All I wanted was to lie next to Eric safe in his arms, to be in that place where only he and I existed, comforting him in his time of need and feeling his love. But I was alone and it hurt. I reminded myself that this was his time of mourning; I needed to be there for him and once again adopt my familiar role in which my needs didn't matter. I reminded myself that I had made this choice; this is what I had "signed up for," and I could continue to be strong. It was now evident to me why my love for Eric was so deep; without it, I would never be able to make it through my own pain and help him with his.

Eric came home a little after 3:00 AM. He slid into bed and said, "I feel good about what I did; I needed to do this. I sat there holding her hand, telling her I loved her and that it was OK to go. I really thought she would pass tonight, but I guess tonight is not the night." He held me and drifted off to sleep. I lay there thinking about what the days ahead would bring as I joined him in sleep.

⟡

The next day, Saturday, we went to see Gaye again. She looked the same; there was no change from the day before. As we watched her lifeless eyes stare at the ceiling, we teared up for her and her struggle. Then, all of the sudden, Gaye's eyes filled with life! She seemed to be looking at someone. Her eyes darted to the wall that was away from Eric and I; her eyes danced and she looked as though she were recognizing someone there that we couldn't see.

I turned to Eric, who had a look of surprise on his face, and said, "She sees someone, Eric! Perhaps her grandparents, I don't know, but she sees someone."

"I'll bet you're right," he said as he looked at his wife.

As quickly as her eyes had filled with life, the vitality left them again. Somehow, Gaye looked different after the incident, but it was heartwarming to know that there would be someone there to help her in her transition to her new life; I felt blessed to have witnessed it.

As we prepared to leave, Eric bent over his wife and kissed her forehead, and as always, it was a special moment that I loved being a part of.

We left and went to get a bite to eat; neither of us was hungry but knew we needed to keep up our energy. After dinner, as we sat in the car in the parking lot of the restaurant, Eric asked if I was OK. The pain that I couldn't manage to mask showed on my face, making it obvious that something was bothering me.

"Yes, I'm OK. I just want to share something with you and it's difficult to get it out," I told him.

After a few moments of tears, I finally said, "Last night was the last night you will ever spend with Gaye. I'm so glad you did it."

We both cried as we clung to each other and agreed that it was bittersweet. I told him he should embrace the gesture and his last moments with his beloved. But I also advised him to remember the Gaye that he had locked in his heart and mind. That was the Gaye I wanted him to remember whenever he thought of their last night together—the Gaye who had danced in her new blouse.

CHAPTER 16

LOVE AND HER SAILOR

Sunday morning, things felt strained. Emotions were taking their toll on us, and in some vague way, we seemed to be angry at each other. Though we didn't admit it aloud, we were waiting for the phone to ring.

I had a baby shower to attend that afternoon for my girlfriend, but I was in no mood to go. I arranged to drop off her gift early. I sat there telling her of the events of the past week. She lent a sympathetic ear but had little to say except that she was sorry for my pain. What does one say in a circumstance such as this? It felt good to get out and talk to someone new. I could see by the look on her face that she empathized. I gave her the gift and returned home.

I got back home and found that Eric was not up to visiting the nursing home. I went in his stead and was not prepared for what I saw. I entered Gaye's room to find her eyes fixed open; she was nasal flaring and tracheal tugging—signs that she was having difficulty breathing. Yet, oddly, she seemed at peace, as if she wasn't fighting death anymore but embracing it. I felt that she wasn't "there"; I felt that she had already gone somewhere else, and her body was just functioning like a machine, still doing what it was programmed to do. I broke down. I wept like a baby. My tears were for sadness at a life cut too short, for the suffering that she had endured—the suffering that she might or might not have been aware of. I also had tears of joy for Gaye. Soon she would be rid of that wretched body forever and the hateful disease would no longer be able to rob her of anything else.

I also cried tears for my own pain at losing the woman I had grown to love, and whose passing I grieved. I never knew her before her illness; I met her when the illness had already invaded her mind and body. But the love I had for her grew from her children, family and Eric. She was mother to the children, and grandmother to the grandchildren, that I now loved. She was the wife of the man that I had devoted my life to and loved with my entire being. How could I not love her?

I sat there, holding her hand and crying. Her hands were ice cold. I checked her feet; although there was no mottling or imminent signs of death, they were ice cold too. I bundled up her hands and feet as best I could to try and warm them and sat down to cry even more. How could this be fair? Not only was Gaye stripped of her memory at a young age, but now she was facing death far too early. As I sat there at her bedside, I spoke to her of seeing family members on the "other side" and of riding horses again. I cried even harder. How was this happening? She was supposed to be with Eric. They were supposed to be living in Europe with children and grandchildren making visits.

I felt anger toward God at that moment. Why was this happening? I know God has a plan, but this seemed like a very bad plan and extremely unfair. No it didn't *seem* unfair—it was unfair! I finally regained my composure, kissed Gaye on the forehead and left the room. I spoke with the nurse and asked how long she thought it would be. "It's so hard to tell," she said. "I've seen it go on for days or just minutes." I thanked her and left. I got in the car, called Eric and broke down again. "Are you OK, hon?" he asked.

"Yes, it's just so hard to see this happening to someone we love so much," I told him.

"Just get home," he said.

As I started driving, I called Mel and left her a message—tearful but with the facts. I needed to talk to someone of my pain. I tried calling my sister. I went to a text conversation we'd had a few days ago, hit her name on the text message, and hit call.

I was puzzled when the call was answered. The voice didn't sound like my sister's. "Who is this"?

"It's me, Joan; you called me, remember"? Joan is a faithful child of God with whom I worked. I explained to her how I tried to call my sister for some spiritual guidance but got her instead.

"I guess I was supposed to call you," I told her.

After we chitchatted, she said, "Just feel his love."

It was what I needed to hear. Ashamed of my anger, I said a prayer for forgiveness for questioning God. It was then that I felt his embrace and realized I could do this. I wasn't alone; I could do this. As I hung up, my phone returned to the conversation my sister and I had, and it didn't display Joan's name or number at all. I found out, later, that my sister would have been unavailable; she was at a function involving her job. The Lord knew what I needed, and he took care of it. I knew right then that he would take care of me during this whole ordeal. I just needed to give him my heart and know he was taking care of me so that I could take care of everyone else.

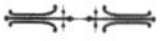

I arrived home and sobbed in Eric's arms. I finally found the strength to tell Eric that I would be surprised if Gaye lived through the night. We awoke the next morning with no phone call. Even in our sleep, we seemed to be waiting for the phone to ring. We went through our routine of getting ready for the day. Eric left for work, while I wondered what would happen if I needed to leave work early. We had been shorthanded lately and were scheduled to have a staff meeting during lunch, so I wasn't sure how I could get away.

Once at work, I realized we didn't have a lot of appointments scheduled, and I began formulating a plan. I was contemplating leaving work briefly so that I could be at the nursing home by eleven thirty and back by twelve thirty for the staff meeting.

I was just getting ready to talk to the MAs about my plan when the receptionist walked into the lab and said, "Eric is on line two." I looked at her; we both knew.

In a flat voice, Eric said, "The nursing home called; they say she's going."

"I'll be there as soon as I can," I told him. I informed my boss and the MAs and left as soon as I could. During my drive, I was deep in thought and prayer. Later on, Eric told me that while he drove to the nursing home, he wondered if it was another "false alarm." He had been called to the nursing home on several occasions in this way and wondered if this would be more of the same. He hoped not.

When I arrived in Gaye's room, the chaplain was reading scriptures and praying with her. There was soft music playing in the background. It was very peaceful. The chaplain looked up at me and smiled with loving eyes and moved from the chair so I could sit with Gaye. I sat there, holding her cold hand, watching the last few breaths she would ever take. I told her to feel God's love. It was all around us, and soon she would be with the loved ones who had passed before her.

Then it happened—she stopped breathing. I was frightened; I wanted Eric to be with her when she passed.

I pleaded with her, "Eric is on his way, he'll be here soon. Gaye, he'll be here any minute. Please wait for him."

After about a minute or two with no breaths from Gaye, the Chaplain whispered that she would go get the nurse. But then with what seemed like a lot of effort from her, she took another breath and the rhythmic breathing started again. A few minutes later, Eric was at the door. I wasn't sure that he would want to see her this way, as she didn't look like his wife at all. She didn't even look anything like the woman he had stayed the night with just three days before. I stopped him.

"Is she really going?" he asked with fear on his face.

"Yes, she's not going to be here much longer," I told him.

He began to weep. I asked him if he wanted to see her. He said he did, and I warned him about her changed appearance. He still said yes and we went in. He later shared with me that he was in shock when I told him she was finally passing, that he almost couldn't believe it.

As we neared her bedside, he broke down again. We stood there holding each other, sobbing, then walked closer to her. When he got a better look at her, he turned to me with an expression of horror on his face; I motioned him to sit down and acted as though everything was fine. I asked if he wanted to hold her hand. He said yes then took her hand and spoke sweetly to her. "It's OK, Gaye, it's all going to be OK. I love you and everything is going to be OK now."

And then, with her husband holding her hand, she took her last breath. She was finally free from that cursed body.

The chaplain went to get the nurse to confirm her passing. After the nurse listened to her lifeless body, she looked up at Eric and nodded. "She's gone."

We stood there, holding each other again, crying. Gaye was no longer to suffer in that body and, once again, would have memories of her life.

As we began to leave the room, Eric took his phone from his pocket to call Mel. As I walked beside him, the chaplain pulled me back into the room and said, "If I hadn't seen it, I would never have believed it," she said.

"What?" I asked.

"Gaye left soon after you arrived. We both saw it. When you mentioned her husband was coming, she decided to wait. You can't tell me you didn't see that," she said.

"I did. The spirit is a powerful thing, you know that as well as I do. Gaye knew Eric needed to be with her when she left, so that's why she came back for him. I feel that it was her way of telling him that she loves him. I will never forget that memory for as long as I live; it was a gift from her, for both Eric and me." The chaplain nodded and I left her to join Eric.

When Gaye passed away, she was only fifty-six years old but didn't even slightly resemble the vibrant, beautiful woman she had once been. When we were in the car and Eric had finished his phone call to Mel, I pleaded with him, "Please don't remember her like that. I need you to remember her in the way that you loved her. Her body gave out long before it was supposed to, so promise me you'll try and remember the Gaye you loved, not the one you just said good-bye to."

He said he would do his best; he, too, didn't want to remember that person lying in the bed, who was less than a shadow of the wife he'd known. I described the moments before he arrived, and how Gaye had waited for him, returning to be with him so that he could be near her during her passing.

We held each other in the car, weeping, trying to figure out what was next. Mel would know what to do; she was on her way from Pueblo with Jamie. She would know what to do.

CHAPTER 17
PROGRESSING

Mel and Jamie came up that afternoon to be with Eric. After a light lunch, while I attended to the dishes in the kitchen, they settled in the living room. I was so thankful that Eric had Melanie. She has been his strength for such a long time.

Eric would call her five to six times a day, before he met me. As a matter of fact, she has commented several times, in jest, about how her dad used to call her all the time, but since he met me, she was lucky to hear from him once a month. But she always adds that she is happy that "he has a life now" and isn't upset about the lack of phone calls. She's told me a dozen times that she wouldn't have it any other way.

But I know what Mel was to her dad. More than just strength to lean on, she was company in his otherwise lonely world. Her family, her boys and Jamie, were always so supportive when Mel's father called on her. Their patience in sharing her is to be admired. They all knew Eric needed their mom and wife and hoped that it would soon come to an end.

It wasn't too long ago that Mel confided in me that she and her mom, before the illness, were finally in a place where they were getting along and forming a wonderful bond. One that she never thought would happen while she was going through her rebellious teen years. In the years just before the illness, Mel and Gaye would call each other as the holidays approached to discuss what creative things they were interested in making for that year. They were both artistic: Gaye with her painting, doll making and quilting; and Mel with her painting, sewing and cake decorating. They were a lot alike but different in many ways as well. My heart ached for her when she told me this. To lose your mother, just when you were really forming the relationship you've always craved, was heartbreaking.

Melanie, along with Emily, had been instrumental in finding the nursing home for Gaye. Mel had also helped Eric get insurance to pay for the nursing home and was Eric's emotional support through the toughest of times; without her, Eric would surely have crumbled. Watching them on the couch now, his arm tenderly wrapped around her shoulders, was a moving sight. They were feeling their pain and sharing in their grief, supporting each other. They were allowing each other to feel relief without guilt as they remembered the woman Gaye was. "I won't intrude," I thought to myself. Once again, I felt that this was their time; I wanted them to share the moment completely, in its purest form.

As I finished the dishes, I overheard their discussion about what the plans would be. There would be a memorial service here at our house; then there would be a burial in Idaho, with the date to be determined later. They spoke of relief that it was all over and that Gaye was in a much better place. I excused myself to the bedroom. I needed to write of this moment and of the love I felt. I needed to get the flurry of emotions I was feeling down on paper as well as the emotions I was witnessing. Writing, at the time, seemed to be the best way for me to work through my own pain in order to help with theirs.

After about thirty minutes, Eric came into the bedroom and asked, "Hon, why aren't you out here with us?"

"I feel like this is your time together. You need to be supporting each other and feeling your pain. You don't need me to muddle things up. Really, everything is fine; this is your family's time," I told him.

"But I want you out there; please, come out here," he pleaded. I looked into his eyes and saw the pain he was feeling and told him I needed to wrap up my writing and I'd be out shortly.

A few minutes later I joined them in the living room. Eric was, again, sitting on the couch with Mel, so I took the chair at the other end of the couch, across from Jamie. The tenderness in each of their eyes was so endearing; there was pain, but I sensed more relief than anything. The roller coaster ride was over. The suffering for Gaye was done. They could truly move on.

They discussed the coming days and what needed to be done. The funeral home needed to be visited. Eric said he would go tomorrow. Melanie said she would go with him, and he agreed. I told Eric I could get off work and go if he'd like. He said it wouldn't be necessary, that he and Mel could work it all out. Those words hurt. I understood them, but they still hurt. I felt as though I needed to be with him, but apparently it wasn't what he needed, so I gathered up my hurt emotions and packed them safely in the place where they belonged.

Truly, in my mind, I knew that it was Eric and Mel who needed to attend to the details together; it would be part of their healing. Sometimes, simply going through the motions of what must be done can help one with the pain of losing family. Even though I felt that I was a part of Gaye's family, for I loved her and her family dearly, I sensed that I was being reminded that I was "not family."

As the conversation went on, I offered suggestions a couple of times—only to be "shut down" by Mel. I understood. It was her mom; she needed to be in control of the decision making. She would handle it all, for her mom.

I sat there the rest of the time, silently listening. Gaye's memorial would be the coming Sunday. Eric would find an appropriate picture, order the food and come up with pictures for the Power Point with music that would play on the TV during the gathering. He would also notify friends and family of the service. Melanie had a poem she wanted to read and a prayer she wanted to say. The plans were made; Melanie knew just what to do, and we were lucky to have her. We were also fortunate that a lot of the decisions had been made prior to Gaye's passing. The trip to the funeral home the week before proved invaluable and if Mel hadn't been there to make sure her father stayed to take care of the arrangements, there would have been a lot more to deal with. Mel's strength and wisdom were a godsend.

Eric motioned for me to join him on the couch. I begged off because I felt that Melanie needed her dad. He was persistent. Finally, Mel said, "He needs you; come over here."

I reluctantly joined them on the couch, comforting him in an unfamiliar way. Not really knowing what to do to make him feel better, I let him say what he needed and touch me how he needed. Mel seemed a bit angry at me and snapped at me a couple of times. I took no offense. She was hurting; the stings served to remind me of that. She had just lost her mother and I felt I was in the way of her being with her father, the exact reasons I didn't want to intrude on their space. The plans being made, Mel and Jamie left for home.

The next morning, knowing that Eric had to venture to the funeral home to make the final arrangements, I found myself feeling lost. I knew how Eric felt about me going to the funeral home with him, but I couldn't bear the idea of not being near him for at least a little while, even though I knew I had to work.

As we cuddled in bed, I asked, "Will you be done in time to meet me for lunch?" I was hopeful that I would get to see him at some point during the day.

We agreed to meet at the Mexican restaurant across the street from my office. I felt better; I couldn't be with him all day, but I could be with him for a portion of it. We went to get coffee before I had to be at work. He was far away in thought, understandably so. I got to work, feeling a bit sorry for myself at having to be there, and tried desperately to shake the selfish thought from my head. Later on that morning, I called to check on Eric. He told me that he and Mel would be there at twelve thirty for lunch.

He and Mel? I love Mel, but I wanted and needed to be with him, by myself. I knew that in the coming days, I would have to share him with so many people, and that he would belong to Gaye and to everyone else. I was looking forward to lunch with him by myself this one last time before things got too complicated.

"Oh, I forgot about Mel; it seems silly that you'd have to come all the way up here and then she'll have to go all the way back down to Pueblo. No, you do what you need to do, have lunch in town with Mel, and I'll see you tonight."

That killed me to say, but I realized that he and Mel needed to be together, more than I needed to be with him. He could hear my self-pity on the phone. I tried to hide it, but he heard my pain and wouldn't hang up until I had explained myself.

Finally, after looking for the right words, I admitted to wanting to have him to myself both for his comfort and my own. But I also assured him that I understood his obligations at this time.

A little while later, Eric called again. "I phoned Mel and told her it was silly for her to come up here from Pueblo for a ten-minute appointment at the funeral home and then go home. Instead, I want her to find out how we go about setting up donations for the Alzheimer's association and to call the nursing home to see if they can find the picture we had in Gaye's room in the Alzheimer's unit.

I think Donnie would like to have it. I'll be up to meet you for lunch at twelve thirty."

Embarrassed at being so selfish, I felt the flush of redness on my face. What was wrong with me? Why was I feeling so needy? I was ashamed of my neediness and realized then that this was going to be a battle for me.

Eric came into the office a little before twelve thirty and we walked over to the restaurant. Once seated, I broke down and apologized for being so selfish. Eric reassured me. "It worked out well this way, and we need to take care of you in all this too."

I felt much better. Though still uncomfortable about being selfish, I also believed that we both needed to be connected at this particular time.

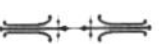

That evening, we went to the nursing home. They had the picture that Mel had called about and a lot of other stuff that they said was Gaye's. We decided to donate all but the picture to the residents of the nursing home.

As we were leaving, Eric paused at the front door. "This will, quite possibly, be the last time I ever come here," he said.

"So how does that make you feel?" I asked.

"Relieved, actually," he said, "very relieved."

The next evening Eric and I went to the store to order the deli trays for the service. Once we got back home, I took Eric downstairs to show him a few pictures I had rummaged through. I had picked a few that I thought were great pictures of Gaye. He chose one, actually my favorite, of Gaye smiling. She was in the sunshine, looking like she was having a great day; it was a beautiful picture. We both stood there staring at her happy face, a face and a mind that were healthy and intact—before the disease reared its ugly head and invaded her and her family.

"Do you remember this day?" I asked Eric, finally breaking the silence.

"No, but I really do like this picture," he told me with a wavering smile on his face.

"I like it because she's smiling and outside. You always told me how she was an 'outdoorsy' kind of person. This really is beautiful," I told him.

We spent every evening working on the plans for the memorial. When we weren't busy, and finally able to sit and relax, I would ask Eric to recall favorite memories of Gaye. I hoped that in doing so, and sharing them with me, he would strengthen his recollection of the good times and forget the memory of the woman lying in the bed. He told me again of their meeting and recounted stories of the children, his and Gaye's life together and the special times they'd most enjoyed. As he talked, he would get lost in the world of his memories. Sometimes he smiled; at other times, remembering brought a tear to his eyes and made his voice catch. I will forever cherish the time that we sat there, sharing memories and thinking of Gaye; it was as though we held our own private memorial for her.

As the week wore on, I began to realize that I was dreading Sunday. It would be a trial to witness the pain on everyone's faces. To add to the difficulty, this would be the first time since Christmas that I would see Emily and Megan, and I had no clear idea how to act around them. I worried that I would feel lost in a sea of people whom I might not know, wondering how they knew Gaye and if they knew about me.

My heart ached for the family and friends that would be coming to pay their condolences to Eric. It ached for Gaye's children and grandchildren. It ached for myself, as I, too, had loved Gaye and was grieving. But, most of all, my heart ached for Eric and Gaye.

They should be together, sharing time with their family and friends, not attending a memorial, one for the other. It shouldn't be this way; it seemed so unfair and it broke my heart. I knew that during the day there were going to be painful things happening, and words spoken that would hurt, but the memorial was part of the whole ordeal. I would have to be strong, for myself and for Eric. I could do this.

Once, during an especially hard time a few months ago, Mark told me, "You're the strongest person I know, Mom; you can do this." I wasn't sure that I could live up to that statement, but there was nothing I could do at this point. I was here for Eric, his family and Gaye; this is what our lives had revolved around over the past few years. This chapter was coming to an end, and I was here doing what needed to be done…for everyone.

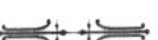

Looking back on the difficult time before the memorial, I can't help wondering if anyone really understood what I was going through as the "other woman." Some friends that I confided in tried to empathize and theorized that I had taken on such a difficult role because I was a nurse at heart, as well as by profession. Perhaps it took a nurse to be able to withstand what I endured, for a nurse is a selfless person and can be strong during the worst of times. If I hadn't been a nurse at heart, no doubt I would have packed my things and run a long time ago—and spared myself a lot of pain.

I've come to the realization that it was partly because I am a nurse that I was attracted to Eric. But it wasn't why I fell in love with him. This I do know: Our love was meant to be, and for whatever reason, it just happened that the love of my life needed me long before he could truly be mine. I am a patient person, and I waited my turn. And maybe it's because of who I am that I was able to "stick it out" and hang on for the future.

The morning that Gaye passed away, before we had word of anything, I had confided in Gloria, a colleague at the office and someone I considered a friend. "I am here for Eric; I move aside and let his family have their time when they need it. I am here for the family. But it seems as if no one gets that I am hurting too, for Eric of course, but for myself as well. Why doesn't anyone realize what it means to be in love with a man who is still in love with his wife? When I see Eric's tenderness and love for Gaye, I admire and cherish it but also want it for myself. After all, I am a woman, not a saint!"

Gloria said what so many of my friends had said: "I understand, but I don't know how to help you with the pain." Then she added, "Just keep remembering why you're with him, though. You belong with him. He's what you've looked for your whole life, and he loves you so much; I can tell by the way he looks at you. You are his world."

I knew she was right; Eric was—and is—the man of my dreams, the love of my life. And in the past, I had feared that such a man only existed in my dreams. I was so grateful to Gloria for reminding me of the love I had. I kept her words close to me and would lean on them during the memorial. I could do this, I knew I could.

CHAPTER 18
THE MEMORIAL

The day before the memorial, Eric and I went to shop for fresh flowers for display at the gathering. While at the florist, Eric saw some bleeding hearts. "Gaye loved bleeding hearts," he reminded me.

"Then we'll get a plant for each of the kids. Rix and Mel can plant them and enjoy them every year, knowing that Gaye loved them so much," I told him. He agreed.

The next day would be a busy one. I began, early, getting everything ready; I wanted the memorial to be meaningful to everyone coming. I placed Gaye's picture on a table near the entryway with a candle and a vase with wild flowers next to it. It was a beautiful tribute to a beautiful spirit, I thought.

Over on the sofa table I had the two bleeding heart plants for Mel and Rix; I hoped they would be pleased with the sentiment. The pictures were loaded, via flash drive, onto the TV in the great room; pictures of Gaye and her life faded in and out as some of her favorite music played gently in the background. It was all a very beautiful and heartfelt testimonial to her, one I think she would have embraced.

Eric and I were finishing up getting ready in the bedroom when he came to me with his wedding band in his hand. "This will be the last time I wear this," he said with tear-filled eyes as he slid it onto his ring finger. We embraced and wept. It was a beautiful sentiment and testimony of their marriage. He wanted to give Gaye one last day of being her husband and to show her the love he had for her. Their almost thirty-four year marriage had been over a long time ago in Eric's mind, and now, except for his last tribute to their love, it was "officially" over. I wept for the tenderness of the moment and for his pain. I wept for my own pain as well, for I was being reminded that I was not his "chosen one." But, in all honesty, my tears were because the one he had first loved would not be a part of his life anymore—and not by his choice. In a perfect world he would still be with Gaye.

We continued to hold each other, and then the phone rang. It was Mel; her family and Rix's would be arriving soon. It was going to be a sad and painful greeting; I didn't want to be in the way. I didn't want the family to feel that they had to present pleasantries to me and Amanda; it was their time to grieve and I decided I wouldn't be in the way. They should have their first meeting since Gaye's death alone, without an "outsider."

I told Eric that I would go to the store and pick up the deli trays. "But Mel and Rix are arriving soon; don't you want to be here?" he asked.

"No, I need to get the trays; it won't be long before everyone starts arriving. And besides, you need to be with your family right now."

"You are my family," he reminded me.

As we stood at the deli counter, tears welled up in my eyes.

"What's the matter, Mom?" Amanda asked.

"Nothing. I'm just feeling pain and I don't like thinking about it," I told her.

"Mom, if it bothers you, you should talk about it," she said in the same tone I would have used with her.

When I was finally able to choke back my tears, I told her, "Eric has chosen to wear his wedding ring today; it's a beautiful sentiment and I love that he is keeping the love of their marriage alive this way. But it's things like this that remind me of who I am in his life, so it hurts."

"What do you mean? You guys live together, you're sharing your life together, and someday you'll be married. You are his life partner now," she said, obviously confused.

"Yes, you're right. But what I am reminded of is that Eric should be with Gaye. That she is the one that he chose to be life partners with. It hurts me as a woman with these feelings, but it also hurts me that his dreams are shattered and he is not with the one he planned his life with. His pain is my pain, I feel it so deeply for him," I told her with tears streaming down my face.

"Tell him not to wear it," she said as only a fourteen-year-old could understand it.

"I would never do such a thing. Wearing the ring is not what my pain is about; it's about what it signifies. It's the end of their life together, the end of their dream. I think it's beautiful and I am proud of him that he has such devotion to have thought of it. It's one of the reasons I love him so much. Taking off the ring wouldn't change anything, and it's a beautiful way his children can see how much he loves their mother," I said, trying to help her understand.

At that moment, she got a look on her face as though things "hit her" all of the sudden, as if she realized the varied emotions I'd had to endure through this journey.

She hugged me and said, "It'll be alright, Mom, it's almost over." We embraced, standing there at the deli counter, and I was so thankful that I had my beautiful daughter with me. Her light would help give me strength today.

Eric later described the greeting of his family as "somber." Everyone met with hugs, but the usual banter of excitement from everyone during a gathering was missing. The children were unusually solemn, with no chitchat about school or what had been going on since the last visit. Even little Brian was quiet. Eric surmised that everyone's initial feelings of relief when Gaye passed away had subsided, and now everyone was pained by the realization that Gaye, their mother, grandmother and wife, had actually died. No longer would they speak or think of her in the ways to which they had become accustomed over the past few years. Now, she was truly gone, in mind, body and spirit.

Once Amanda and I arrived home with the food, we began to carry it into the house. The oldest grandsons greeted Amanda and me at the door with sad, but warm, hugs. They grabbed the deli trays and helped set them up on the dining room table. Rix's family arrived with Emily's parents. We all said our hellos and hugs were exchanged. Megan, as well as Emily, seemed cold and distant. I greeted them both with a warm hello but decided to forego a forced hug from either of them.

Megan barely made eye contact with me. I worried that she might think I shouldn't be here. Perhaps she thought I was trespassing on her family. I was, in her mind, a person taking her grandfather from her grandmother. I decided to respect her feelings by not engaging her; I'd leave any contact up to her.

Amanda, sensing Megan's behavior, decided that she too wouldn't engage her. She and Megan got along well usually, when together; but Amanda was upset about the situation last Christmas and had formed a "not so favorable" opinion of her. I could "read" Amanda's demeanor; she was there for me, to support me in my time of need and, in her young eyes, that meant not engaging someone who had caused her mother pain. After some uncomfortable moments of my helping Emily find what she needed to finish the salad she had prepared, the doorbell rang. I had an escape.

I greeted the first of the guests, Eric's parents. They had flown in from Arizona. I greeted them with warm hugs, thanked them for coming, and explained that it meant the world to Eric that they had come.

Within what seemed like a few minutes there was a flurry of people coming in with warm words of sentiment and condolences. Most didn't seem to know quite what to say. What does one say in a situation such as this? "I'm glad she's finally passed away." "Her suffering's over now." "You must feel a heavy burden has been lifted." Are any of these sentiments the "correct" thing to say in such a situation? It was difficult for some, but it meant the world to us both that each and every one of them took time out of their busy day to come and pay their respects to Eric and Gaye.

Watching Eric, my heart ached for him and all that he was feeling. I'd see his lip tremble and a tear roll down his cheek. I'd immediately come to his side and touch him to give him strength and comfort.

There were questions, mostly directed at me, while Eric was not at my side. I understood the need. Everyone knew that I was with Gaye the day she died and that I could possibly answer any questions they might have. It was safer for them to ask me, so as not to cause Eric any further pain.

At one point during the memorial, Madlyn voiced concern about what I was having to deal with. She led me away from the group of people we were standing with and asked, "How are you doing?"

"We're doing OK," I said. "Eric has his moments; I encourage him to feel everything but try to get him to relive the good memories."

"No," she said, pointing to my chest, "I am asking how *you* are doing?" She continued, "This is a tough time for everyone, but tough for you because of a lot of other reasons. You are a strong human being, but you are a woman and I can only imagine how this all must be taking a toll on you."

There, at last, was the first person from my new family to really voice a concern about me and my feelings. I felt comforted by her warm words. This is when I realized that even though we had spent little to no time together, she genuinely cared about how I felt. I thanked her and assured her I was fine. It was a gift to realize that she seemed to have some insight into what I was going through. I appreciated it far more than she will ever know.

Since meeting Eric's family, his children, and Gaye's family, I have never felt that there was anyone who was concerned about me and my feelings. For the most part, everyone was happy that Eric was happy and that someone was seeing to his needs while he went through such a horrific time. I had always felt as if I was accepted into the family when things were complicated, but for a specific role. But, up to this point, I'd never felt that they genuinely cared about me or my feelings as a person on this journey as well.

My presence, in their minds, seemed to be as "Eric's supporter." I always had felt that they viewed me as a person without my own feelings about the situation, because I had not known Gaye before her illness. But I recognized that this was a complicated issue; there are no books on how to deal with a situation such as ours, and not many people have been put in my position.

I like to think that we were all learning, though not, perhaps, in time to change anything for ourselves and our particular situation. But I hope that we will rely on the skills learned from this dilemma to teach others how to deal with similar situations. I could only hope and pray that things would eventually change, and that I would, someday, be seen as someone who cared for and loved Gaye as well.

The time we all spent together during the memorial was as pleasant as it could have been under the circumstances. At one point, Melanie read a beautiful poem that she'd written and said a prayer for her mother. Expressing the heart and soul of a daughter in pain at losing her mother, her words were genuine, beautiful, and very moving. But I know from

Melanie's thoughts about the day, which she later shared with me, that her pain was from the past. Mel later confided in me that, on the day of the memorial, she felt "removed" from the situation. Many years before the memorial, she had said good-bye to the mother she had known and loved. She also experienced some guilt for feeling a sense of relief on that day, relief that her father was now able to get married, move on and put the past where it belonged. She expressed love and loyalty for her mother but also admitted that, for her, the years of pain she had endured were put to rest when her mother was finally gone.

I chose to share the beautiful story of Gaye's passing with only a few close friends and Madlyn. I recalled how she "came back" so that her beloved could be by her side when she passed, both for his peace and, perhaps, to hear his voice one last time. Everyone who heard the story was truly moved by it, and it's one I will treasure for the rest of my life; I was so blessed to have been a witness to it. After hearing the story, Madlyn said, "Of course she waited; I know Gaye and I believe she waited for Eric just as you described it!"

The beautiful memorial, given by a family who loved her and celebrated her life, was coming to an end. As family and friends began to leave, the house quieted down. Eric's children and grandchildren remained. We sat in the living room and chatted. Megan, who had seemed to avoid me most of the day, finally made a gesture of friendship and perhaps of acceptance. I felt her watch me, several times, throughout the day; but I continued to give her the space I felt she wanted. Just before Rix and his family were leaving, she took a seat on the arm of the chair I was sitting in. As Emily and Rix called their family to get ready to leave, Megan put her arms out for a hug. I was so moved that I actually had to fight tears as I embraced her. I hoped that in the few minutes I held her, she could feel the love that I had for her and for her grandmother. In any event, I basked in the gesture and felt at peace with her.

After everyone left, I finished up the dishes and put the leftover food away. I was exhausted, emotionally and physically. I sat next to Eric on the couch and snuggled up against him. After a few moments, I looked up at him and asked, "So how are you feeling?"

"It was a good day; I feel really good about the whole thing," he told me with a sad, but genuine, smile. I kissed his cheek and excused myself to the bathroom.

Now that it was all over and Eric was in a good place, I needed to take care of me. There was a lot I needed to process, without Eric feeling any added pain from me; the bathroom seemed like a good place to escape to. With the closing of the door behind me, I felt the dam break. I fought with all my might but could no longer hold back the flow of my tears. I wept like a young child who had fallen and scraped her knee. I kept my tears quiet, not wanting to burden Eric with anything else. I wept and wept, hoping I would feel better when I was done, but I couldn't get done. I felt as though I could cry forever.

When I finally thought I could compose myself enough to conceal my feelings, I wiped my eyes, put a smile on my face, took a deep breath and opened the door to find Eric standing there waiting for me, obvious pain on his face.

"Why are you crying? And why aren't you sharing it with me?" he asked.

"I wasn't crying, I'm fine," I lied.

"You can't lie to me. What is it?" he insisted.

I insisted that it wasn't important.

"If it's important enough for you to cry, then I need to know about it," he said, holding me in a tight embrace.

I broke down and couldn't hide my emotions from him anymore. "I just feel so much pain and for so many different reasons. From you wearing your wedding ring, which is the sweetest thing I've ever witnessed, to the loss of a person I truly loved, and then to feeling like an outsider because no one knows I am grieving for Gaye as well. Those feelings mixed with all of the stuff in between: the kids' pain, the grandchildren's pain, Ila losing her child, and Gaye— poor Gaye— she didn't deserve this; you both didn't deserve this. Everyone looks at me as someone who didn't even know Gaye, so why would I grieve for her? But I do grieve. I grieve for everything about her. I grieve for you and her losing your lives together, for her having to leave her family, and for her dying of that wretched disease. But no one sees that—to them, I am just the girl who is expected to hold Eric up. I'm bleeding too. I love Gaye and everyone who loves her, but no one seems to realize this," I told him through my sobs.

"I know," he said. "I know what you have been to me, and what you are to Gaye and her memory, what you are to her family, and to her children. I know you love her; your passion for her is obvious in everything you've done for me and for her. You've made me visit pain, love and joy in reliving my memories of her. I know your pain, hon, really I do. I'm sorry it's been so hard on you. Know that I love you and that I'm here for your pain as well," he said with tear-filled eyes.

I know he was aware of my grief, but somehow I still felt lonely. I did, though, feel a huge relief. Simply by my verbalizing my feelings to him, a burden had been lifted from me.

With this "meltdown" behind me, I would be able to move on and deal with whatever else was to come, and I knew there was still a lot left to face. The burial was planned for June.

CHAPTER 19
ONE LAST DIFFICULT TIME

The weeks following Gaye's death and her memorial were filled with emotion, but there seemed to be a sense of harmony as well. Eric and I continued to discuss Gaye and his good memories of her. There were sad moments, happy moments and moments of reprieve.

Eric, when asked, described an overwhelming feeling of relief that the nightmare was over. Although the burial was still to come, he felt "in a good place" and was ready to move on after everything was said and done.

On a sunny Saturday afternoon in early June, Eric and I were sitting outside enjoying the weather, when Mel called.

"Hey, Tami! How are you guys doing?" she asked in her usual happy tone.

"We're good, just sitting on the upper deck trying to figure out what to do this weekend.

As the conversation progressed, it turned out that Mel had a question for us. After determining that Eric was there at my side, she didn't beat around the bush. "When are you and Dad going to get married?" she asked. The question and the heartfelt excitement in her voice took me by surprise.

I have to admit that in the past few days, since the flurry of all the activity had quieted a bit, I had begun to think about the possibility of Eric and I getting married. I felt it would be helpful for us both to heal and to move on together in a way that would be new and exciting, but I wanted it to be Eric's idea to bring up the subject, when he felt ready.

I looked over at Eric and repeated her question: "She wants to know when we're getting married." Eric smiled as I tried to compose an answer for her.

"Well," I stammered back to her, "we haven't really started talking about it just yet. We don't want to be disrespectful to your mom and their marriage, or to anyone for that matter." I couldn't help thinking of Megan.

"I don't care what anyone thinks, and neither should you; you need to do what you need and want to do. I appreciate the dignity you are giving their relationship, but it's time for Dad to be able to put this all behind him."

I wasn't quite sure what to say at that point. Eric, sensing my unease, piped up so she could hear. "Mel, we'll be talking about it soon and when we have a date, you'll be the first to know."

"I'll be counting on it!" she said. I repeated her words to Eric.

After Mel and I ended our conversation about the boys, nursing school—the usual—she spoke briefly with her father; then they hung up. "So what do you make of that?" I asked him.

"I think it was Mel's way of saying it's OK for us to be talking about marriage," he said with a smile. "She's right, you know. It is OK. Gaye 'died' for me, a long time ago. You and I couldn't marry because she was still physically here. Now that she's not, we should be talking about it," he said as he put his arm around me. "So, when do you want to get married?" he asked me.

"It's not that I haven't thought about it, but I was afraid it was too soon to mention anything," I told him. "I don't know, maybe in six months?" Not sure how he'd react, I made my suggestion sound like question.

"Six months is what I was thinking too. That would make it about October, right?" he asked.

I nodded.

"Well then, how about October thirteenth? The day we met," he added with a grin on his face.

"That's a wonderful idea!" I told him with a hug. "It will be three years to the day we met; we'll have both anniversaries on the same day. Hey, I just realized, you get out of buying one gift that way—you're clever!" I teased.

We embraced again. As I pulled away to look into his eyes, he said, "It is time to move on. It's time to get on with things, the way we need to. It feels good."

"Let's not mention it to anyone until after the burial. We have this one last hurdle to make; I just want to make sure that everyone would be in a better place to hear the news," I explained.

Eric agreed. "We'll wait until the right time to tell everyone, once everything is taken care of. So, we have a date. How do we want to do it?" he asked.

"I'd like a quiet ceremony with just you and me; then perhaps a party afterwards for our friends and family to help us celebrate. Maybe a few days later."

I looked up the date on my phone. "October 13 is on a Wednesday; we could get married then and have a reception on the following Saturday for all of our family and friends. What do you think?" I asked him, feeling my excitement build.

The next thing we had to decide was where to get married. For a few days we went back and forth about possible places: Vegas, Europe, Colorado Springs. We just couldn't make up our minds.

One morning while lying in bed, we were again discussing wedding locales without reaching a decision. Imitating his mother, I finally said in exasperation, "Oh Ray!" (Ray is Eric's middle name and the name his family calls him).

Then it hit me. "Ouray!" I shouted.

Ouray, Colorado—pronounced U-ray—was a place I had visited once and found beautiful. "I'd love to get married there!" I said, excited at the thought.

Eric was deep in thought for a moment. "I've been there," he said. "Yes, we'll go to Ouray to get married. That's the ticket!" He sounded as excited at the thought as I was.

"I'll find a bed and breakfast and see about where to get married," I offered. We hugged each other in anticipation.

There was light at the end of the long tunnel we had been traveling through these past few years. It wouldn't be long until we could really start our lives together, because June 27, the day of the burial, was approaching. That date would mark the end of a long and heart-rending journey.

In the couple of weeks before the service in Idaho, Eric and I relaxed somewhat in the respite before we would have to face the last hurdle that stood between us and moving on with our lives. We went to work as usual and just waited.

"Ila called me today," Eric informed me as I walked in the door from working my Saturday shift at the clinic. She said we can stay at her house during the weekend of the graveside service."

It had been decided that the service would be held in Idaho for the other family members that couldn't travel to Colorado and because Gaye's grandparents, whom she had always been very close to, were buried there.

"She said she'd have to make room for everyone because Mel and her family need a place to stay as well. Mel offered to stay in a motel," he added.

"Honey," I interrupted, "Mel is still in nursing school; I'm sure that she doesn't have the extra money to spend on a motel room for her family. Perhaps you and I should stay in a motel and Mel's family can stay with Ila. What do you think?" I asked him.

"I think that's a great idea. It would do me good to be away from all the 'banter' that will be going on, and we'll have a peaceful place to rest at night. I'll call Mel and she can let Ila know. I know of a great place to stay too— it's on the river there near the falls."

Eric also informed me that Donnie, Gaye's sister, was handling all the arrangements for the service. Due to some issues at the cemetery where Gaye's grandparents were buried, we couldn't have her remains buried there. But Donnie had found a spot that she thought was perfect. It was in Swan Valley, not far from her home, and she could look after her sister's final resting place for everyone.

Gaye's mother, Ila, was having the gravestone made. A few days later, we received an email from her with an attached picture of the gravestone. I said, "It's beautiful Eric, don't you think?"

Eric was silent, and one look at his face told me how hard this was for him.

"I'm sorry, honey, I know this is something no one wants to have to do for a loved one, especially their wife," I said as I wrapped my arms around him, holding him close to me.

Tears streamed down his face as he asked me, "Do you really like it?"

"More importantly, do you think Gaye would have liked it?" I asked him.

He nodded his head, "Yes, I think she would have loved it." He was finally able to choke out the words through tears. "I'll call Mel and make sure she agrees; then she can call Ila and tell her it's a 'go.' It's just so hard for me to have to deal with talking to Ila about this stuff."

I held him for a while, trying to comfort his pain, but how does one do that? How do you take away the pain of making decisions about where your spouse should be buried and what her gravestone should be? I could only do what my instincts told me to do, and that was to hold him while soothing away his pain with gentle kisses to his forehead.

Softly I asked him, "How are you feeling about all this, about the graveside service and seeing the family?"

After a while, his tears receded and he said, "I feel a bit guilty, honestly. I feel like I should be doing something to help out with the arrangements in Idaho. I understand that it's how Gaye's family can feel like they are doing something, one last thing, for Gaye. But I can't help feeling like I should be helping," he explained.

"Is that all?" I asked. "How are your feelings holding up, I mean with all the pain that will be associated with the service and the burial?" I asked him.

After giving it some thought he said, "One last difficult time—it's almost all over...one last difficult time."

Later that afternoon, after Eric had made reservations for our room in Idaho Falls, he called Mel about the gravestone. She agreed it was perfect and that she loved it as well. She also expressed gratitude that she could stay at Ila's house.

"Oh, and Dad, Rix, Megan and Brian will be going, but Emily will be out of the country for business. Rix has a hotel; did you get one yet?" she asked.

Eric told her our plans and asked where Rix was staying. The two continued chatting about the arrangements, until Mel abruptly changed the subject. "Dad, Father's Day is coming up; Rix and I want to take you out to lunch."

Eric was always excited to spend time with his family, and when he hung up, he had a smile on his face that I hadn't seen in a while. Mel and Rix knew what their dad needed; they were coming to be with him and to perhaps check on him. I was delighted that he had been so truly blessed by wonderful children.

Father's Day was a wonderful day. Melanie and her oldest, Nathan, along with Rix, Megan and Brian, all arrived around 11:00 AM, Father's Day morning. Treats for the grandkids and a couple of games of pool put everyone in great spirits.

Mel and I chatted about the graveside service. "I really don't even want to think about it," she said at one point and motioned as if pulling her hair out.

"What's going on?" I asked.

"Donnie wants me to help her rewrite the obituary that she wrote for the paper, because she is going to read it at the graveside service. I really don't have any time or desire to do this."

I understood Mel's feelings on it but saw this as an opportunity to help her realize that there was this one last painful piece. Just as I was going to offer my opinion, the rest of the family decided it was time to go to lunch. While killing time on the "wait list" for a table, we crossed the street and watched Brian play in the park; the day was beautiful and we were all enjoying each other. Lunch was great but the company was even better. Eric later said that he felt a renewed connection with his kids, something he needed desperately at this time.

Eric and I arrived home and settled down for the evening. Things felt strange—detached. I knew that this feeling had to do with the weekend ahead: the burial, the family and all the "stuff" that would go with such an emotionally charged get-together. Eric and I both dreaded the thought of it. Old wounds would be reopened and emotions would be running high; we really didn't want to revisit that pain, but of course it had to be done. Gaye's remains needed to be put where they belonged, and the family needed for it to be truly over so that their healing could begin. Once the pain was buried, the memory of the true Gaye would take over their hearts again.

The days leading up to the burial were tension filled. We were both on edge. When I arrived home after work on Thursday, Eric said, "You look tired."

He was right. I felt really weary but couldn't figure out why, because my day wasn't very busy. After giving it some thought, I realized that it was the stress of the coming weekend. I didn't know how I was going to do it. It was hard enough dealing with everything when Gaye's family wasn't present, but now it was going to be awkward and emotional, because this was about her family.

That evening, as Eric and I sat on the back deck relaxing, he broke the comfortable silence. "Do you know how weird and tense it's going to be for me being around Gaye's family?"

"But you've always gotten along with her family, haven't you?" I asked.

"Yes, of course. I'm just worried that they'll be wondering why I didn't take more of an active role in the service in Idaho. But I feel as if I've done my grieving and my share of what needed to be done by having the memorial," he explained.

"I see what you're saying, but I think you're wrong about that. I don't think that they think about your involvement, or lack of, with the planning of the service at all. They know about the memorial and how it was a beautiful affirmation of your love for Gaye and tribute to her memory. Mel told them all about it through Ila. I really don't think you have anything to worry about. I want you to embrace the time you have with them, though. Promise me you will feel their pain as well as yours. This service is for everyone, including you."

It was then that I began thinking about how uncomfortable this trip would be for me. I was going to have to be around a lot of people I didn't know who were Gaye's family; that was uncomfortable enough, but to think that some of them would be thinking of me as the "other woman" made it almost unbearable.

Feeling the fear build up inside me, I finally said, "Perhaps I shouldn't go. Maybe it would be easier on everyone if I wasn't 'in the way.' After all, this is for Gaye's family and you."

"It would be harder on me if you didn't go. Please tell me you'll go," he said pleading with me.

"Of course I will; I wouldn't make you face this alone. I just wanted you to know that if it made it easier on you, or anyone, I'd be glad to stay home," I said, trying one last time to get out of going.

"No," he said, "you belong with me, and I'll need you." He held me tight as I continued to think about the upcoming trip. Eric didn't need to convince me—all he had to do was just say he wanted me there.

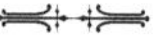

The truth is that Ila and Donnie have never made me feel uncomfortable; they have always welcomed me into their family with warm, open arms; they weren't the ones I was worried about. It was the other friends and relatives who didn't know our situation and who would judge our relationship and, ultimately, judge me. How was I going to do this? I had a feeling it was going to be worse than the memorial service. I would have to be alone a lot; Eric had to be there for the grieving family, because I had decided I would be respectful of them by not interfering. I would have Amanda with me, but she made it clear to me that she would not be going to the graveside service itself. She didn't feel it was a place that she should be; she didn't know Gaye and felt she needed to be respectful and not intrude. I understood and agreed with her.

Because I would have Amanda for most of the visit, the weekend would be bearable. But even if it weren't, I would still be there for Eric.

CHAPTER 20

A CONNECTION FROM BEYOND

I had to work the day we left for Idaho Falls but managed to get out of the office early. I ran a few errands and finally arrived home. I got things ready, called our house sitter and gave her some last-minute instructions. We were on the road later than we wanted to be, but the three of us, Amanda, Eric and I, were all in good spirits. Eric had rented a car so that Amanda would be more comfortable. "The Mini's backseat would be a terrible ride for her all the way to Idaho," he explained.

Gaye's urn was safely packed in the trunk, along with the smaller keepsake urns for the family members who wanted them. Amanda settled down in the backseat with her music, and Eric and I enjoyed conversation. The mood became happy and carefree for all of us; it was almost as though we had forgotten why we were traveling.

We stopped for the night in Rawlins, Wyoming, and started down the road the next morning. As we drove, the reason for our trek remained pushed to the back of our minds. But a while later, I heard the sniffling; I looked up at Eric and I, too, teared up as I tried to comfort him. I held him as best I could while he drove. "Do you want me to drive?" I asked.

He refused my offer and, after a brief pause, I asked him what he was thinking about.

He spent a few moments trying to collect himself and then said, "Gaye and I have driven this road so many times; this is the last time I will ever travel it with her." Our tears flowed.

"He loves her so much; what a heartbreaking reason to have to travel a road once taken with his beloved," I thought to myself. I also thought how lucky Gaye was to have had such great love from her husband; it was certainly the kind you find in love stories.

"What are you thinking about?" he asked me.

"Your pain," I replied through my own tears. After a few minutes, I added, "But I have to tell you, I don't feel like Gaye is in that urn. I never have. I feel that she left her body, for the last time, the day she died and she isn't in that urn. She's here, Eric." I pointed to his heart. "And here," I said as I pointed to his head. "I don't think she wants you to think of her in that urn. And I'm sure she doesn't want you to think of her the way she was over the past seven years. It's the memories of driving this road with her. You and her—with and without the kids—those are the memories you need to hold on to. They are what keep your love and, ultimately, Gaye alive."

He nodded.

"I'd like to pull into a rest area ahead," he said a little while later. "Gaye and I used to stop there every trip to Idaho Falls. There's a pond and a gazebo, and she always said it was her favorite spot to stop when we'd travel this way. I've been thinking about it and I've decided that I'd like to throw one of the little urns in the pond; that way, a part of her is always there," he explained through what seemed like a river of tears.

"I think that's beautiful. Where is it?" I asked.

"We'll be there shortly," he replied. "Should we wake Amanda?"

Amanda, being a teenager who had to get up "early," was fast asleep. I knew Eric would want this to be a sacred moment for himself and Gaye. I wouldn't wake Amanda and, knowing the kind of sleeper she was, I knew she wouldn't wake on her own. I'm sure she'll not even stir while you venture to the pond. If she does—"

"Wait! While 'I' venture to the pond? Aren't you coming with me?" he asked with a look of confusion on his face.

"I just assumed you'd want to be alone with her memory as you took care of the urn," I explained.

"No, I want you with me."

"Of course I'll go with you. I'll not leave you if you that's what you prefer," I assured him.

It wasn't long before we pulled over onto the side of the highway. "I'm pretty sure this is it. The rest area has been closed for quite some time; I'm sure it was a bit expensive to maintain it, so they probably had to shut it down," he explained.

As we got out of the car, I peeked back at Amanda. Closing the car doors didn't stir her a bit. Eric took one of the small urns from the velvet-lined box that held them. There were five small urns in the box, each holding some of Gaye's remains. He looked at me as he held the one he'd chosen close to his chest. His eyes filled with pain.

We walked down toward a gate that was meant to keep out anyone wanting to take refuge there. The road leading to the rest area was tattered and looked like it hadn't been maintained in, as Eric said, a long time. Once in the rest area, we walked on an overgrown dirt trail leading to the gazebo. As we walked up the trail, the pond came into view. "It is beautiful here, Eric. No wonder Gaye loved it so," I said.

He turned to face the pond and stopped. He let go of my hand. "She said it was so peaceful and serene here; that's why she loved it."

I agreed and he suggested that we walk closer to the water.

We inched our way through overgrown bush and found an open area near the pond. We stood there in silence, both of us with tears streaming down our faces. Eric seemed to be going over some thoughts as he pulled the urn from his chest, kissed it ever so gently and tossed it into the water. His tears turned into sobs as he wrapped his arms around me. As we stood there holding each other, sobbing, I said a prayer to Gaye. I prayed that she could be aware of what Eric had just done for her, in her memory and out of the love he held for her. I prayed that, wherever she was, she would know of this sweetest of tributes her beloved husband had paid to her and her memory. Sharing this moment with him and, possibly, Gaye is another dear memory that I will carry for the rest of my life.

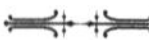

We returned to the car, both of us emotionally exhausted, to find Amanda still sleeping. It wasn't long before we pulled over to a rest area with open restrooms. There were the cutest prairie dogs everywhere around this rest area, and we fed them some treats that we had in the car. It was such a nice diversion from the pain of our last stop. We greatly welcomed little diversions like this. There wouldn't be many over the next two days and we cherished every painless moment that we could.

We had decided to stop to see Donnie, Gaye's sister, on our way to Idaho Falls. We arrived at her house at around two. She was busy with preparations for the service. There were bowls of salads and cut as well as uncut vegetables all over the kitchen. After hugs and greetings and an introduction to Amanda, we sat on the patio as Eric excused himself to the bathroom. I took the opportunity to ask Donnie how she was doing,

"OK. I'm just feeling busy, very busy. There's so much to do," she said, looking exhausted.

"Is there anything I can do to help?" I asked.

"No, most everything is done. I just want to get through this weekend. It's going to be so hard," she said with tears in her eyes. She looked overwhelmed to me, but her new haircut suited her extremely thin frame. I wondered if the "busy" was helping her mask her pain and thought it was not a bad thing to keep "busy."

Eric soon joined us and we left to finish the last forty miles to Idaho Falls.

We arrived at our hotel and admired the view of the falls from our room. It was peaceful as well as beautiful. After a bit of relaxing and getting settled in, we headed over to Ila's house, where everyone was sure to be gathering.

After a warm welcome from Ila, I was introduced to Tina and Gerry. Gerry is Gaye's brother who lives in California and Tina is his wife. They seemed most pleasant and I felt no awkwardness as we chatted. Mel and Rix soon arrived with their families and we all had wonderful conversation, food and togetherness until late into the night. I thought that this part of the family was not, and would never be, uncomfortable. They know that I have genuine love for them all. They have accepted Amanda and me as if we were their own. It was a wonderful feeling to know that we were family to them, but if left to think about it, I would end up feeling sad. If Gaye had not been sick, there would have been no need to "adopt" Amanda and me as family. But on the other hand, because of the circumstances, we had more family to love. I thought, How lucky are we?

After the night of fellowship, we finally decided it was late enough and went back to our hotel. Eric and I sat on the balcony, talking.

"Tomorrow is going to be tough," he said.

"I know, but try and think of it as a sort of celebration. We will all be gathered there thinking and talking about Gaye, not that she was sick. So that, to me, is a celebration. I understand the finality of it all, but try and think of the love that will be there for her," I told him.

"That's just it, it's just so final; that's what is so hard," he replied.

I understood what he was saying; when one has to witness the burial of a loved one, there is a finality to it all. The burial, added to the fact that the sorrow of her passing was still so fresh, was the root of Eric's pain. I felt that even if I tried, I couldn't pull him from his grief. He held on tight to it and must have needed it; I understood and would comfort as best I could. We moved inside and readied ourselves for bed.

As we settled down to sleep, I said an extra prayer. I prayed that I would be able to feel Gaye's presence. I had felt it twice before, in the nursing home, but not in the way I wanted for tomorrow. As I drifted off to sleep, thoughts of Gaye floated in my mind and heart. I had always felt a connection with her since meeting her that first day in the nursing home, and after spending so much time listening to stories from family members about her. The connection deepened with every visit I made to the nursing home. I have a special place in my heart for Gaye and, that night, I hoped that she, her spirit, energy, life force—whatever you want to call it—was in some way able to feel it.

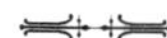

We woke up early, had breakfast, and Eric and I took a walk along the falls while Amanda went back to the hotel room. It was the day of the service, and our conversation, naturally, drifted to what lay ahead in the next few hours. I tried again to help ease Eric's pain with words of encouragement; he wasn't in the frame of mind to accept my suggestions. I am the first one to say that people have to deal with loss in their own way and this, I felt, was his way. I abandoned the fight to steer his feelings away from his grief and, at that point, decided that I would leave him to cope in the way that he needed.

He talked of how unfair life had been to Gaye, how she hadn't deserved to be sick and die so young, and how sad it all was. I let him talk through his tears and pain; he was feeling it all, and it was truly heart wrenching to watch. After what seemed like hours, we were finally able to compose ourselves enough to get Amanda from the room and head over to Ila's.

The atmosphere in Ila's house felt somber and heavy. The looks on everyone's faces spoke volumes—they were not prepared to say good-bye to Gaye but knew they must. The uneasy glances that they exchanged signaled to me that perhaps they needed to share this time, privately, without their adopted family. I excused myself and Amanda and we ventured out to the front yard to let them all be together as they needed. I noticed that there were bleeding hearts blooming everywhere. "Gaye *loved* bleeding hearts," I thought to myself. How beautiful it would be to take some to the service. I decided to pick a bouquet for the angel vase that we'd bought for the memorial. This was something special that I could do for Gaye. Amanda and I got busy gathering bleeding hearts, peonies, Japanese poppy, purple pamida and coral bells. It was a beautiful arrangement, dominated by the bleeding hearts. Gaye loved wild flowers, and I knew that this selection would have delighted her. As I arranged the flowers, Megan came to see what I was doing. "Your grandmother loved bleeding hearts, so I thought she'd love this arrangement at the grave site. What do you think?" I asked her.

"Yes, I think she would," she agreed.

"Would you like to place them during the ceremony yourself? I think she'd love it if you did."

Megan agreed and spoke respectfully, but with obvious pain on her face. She loved her grandmother dearly and was being forced to say good-bye to her before she was ready.

The seating assignments were made for the car trip to the cemetery. First, Eric and I would take Mel's boys and Amanda to the hotel for swimming. Mel's boys felt that they had said good-bye to their grandmother a long time ago and opted not to go to the service. After we left money and instructions with the kids, we headed out to Swan Valley for the final good-byes.

⁂

It was a quiet and uneventful drive. Eric wasn't saying much and a tear rolled down his cheek from time to time; we shared few words. I felt that this was his time for reflecting on what he was having to face, so I sat silently waiting for him to initiate conversation. I held the vase with the arrangement in my lap, admiring how beautiful it was. I kept thinking about Gaye, my heart and mind completely open to her and her memory. We were about three quarters of the way to the cemetery when an odd feeling came over me.

It was as though an inner glow were lighting up my soul. It was almost blinding but, at the same time, it wasn't even there. It was a light like I'd never seen or felt before. It wasn't in front of me, but deep inside of me. It was a warm feeling, one of love and joy.

Then I heard her. "The flowers are beautiful. Thank you for being so thoughtful; I love them."

I was overcome with the warmth that Gaye brought me. I began to tear up, not for sadness, but for joy!

With tears running down my cheeks, I looked over at Eric. With surprise in his voice he asked, "What is it, hon?"

"She's here, I can feel and hear her. Gaye is here, right here, with us."

He looked taken aback.

There was an eerie silence then I said, "She wants you to know that she loves you very much." He looked at me in disbelief; I assured him that I'd heard her say it, as sure as I was sitting there. "She says she knows you're finding it hard to believe me right now, but she wants me to assure you that she is here with us," I explained.

I tried, in my own earthly way, to give her back the love and warmth that she gave me. I could only hope she felt it. But as quickly as she came, she left. I described the feelings and the experience to Eric. I wanted him to believe. I felt her warmth a couple of more times before we reached the cemetery, but she had no more words for me; it seemed she was just letting me know she was near.

The cemetery seemed to be in a strange place. We had to drive through a working farm to get there. But the area was one of the most beautiful, mountainous areas that I had ever seen. From what I've learned about Gaye from her family, she loved to be outdoors in beautiful settings like this. And moreover, Gaye was an accomplished horsewoman who grew up on her grandparents' farm and loved farm life.

"How wonderful," I said to Eric. "Gaye would have picked this spot herself, if she could have! Don't you think?" I asked.

"It's a perfect spot," he agreed.

As we parked the car and walked up to the site, I noticed wildflowers growing everywhere, as if in tribute to Gaye herself. I could think of no better resting place for her remains.

As we approached the grave site, a sad and withdrawn Megan came up to me to take the flowers; she carefully wrapped a yellow ribbon around the stems to hold them together. At the graveside she laid the flowers near the family portrait that someone had placed there before we arrived. The portrait commemorated the last family Christmas that they had all shared before Gaye became so debilitated. It moved me to tears of joy and I hoped that Gaye could feel the love as well.

After we had all gathered around and Donnie had spoken a few words of welcome, Gerry presented a "timeline" of his sister's life. He could barely make it through his reading and I imagined that when he spoke of the unfairness of Gaye's early passing, the reality of it hit him at those moments. It was painful to watch; Eric buried his face deep in my hair and cried. Megan, too, began to weep. I comforted her as best I could with hugs and reassurance.

After the ceremony was done and everyone was milling about and hugging one another, I felt it would be appropriate for me to give the family their space. Brian was growing a bit restless, so I excused us both and took him down to see the bulls in the pasture below the cemetery. On the way, he talked of how fast his shoes made him run and that he was often the fastest runner at school, but that his buddy was sometimes the faster one.

As we approached the bulls, I sensed her presence again. She was enjoying Brian and my tears of joy welled up as, in some deep part of myself, I could actually feel her smiling. Gaye was with her grandson, and I was honored to be part of such an intimate moment.

After the graveside service was over, we all went to the American Legion hall for food and fellowship. Feeling uncomfortable with the stares and whisperings that were directed my way, I escaped from the reception as soon as I could decently manage.

Back at Ila's, Megan asked if Amanda would stay another day with her so she wouldn't be the only girl. Originally, the three of us were to leave the next morning, but Megan suggested that Amanda stay and ride back with them to Longmont, and I could pick her up there. Amanda agreed and Gerry thoughtfully took her back to our hotel to get her things. The girls would stay at Ila's for the night with Mel's family. Megan needed some fun, as the service was hard on her, and I was glad that she and Amanda had renewed their connection.

Once we returned to our room, Eric and I sat on the balcony, soothed by the sound of the falls. He was enjoying a cigar as I took in the view. "I wish *I* could feel her," he said after a period of silence. "I just wish I could believe it all—that she does live on and that she does come to you. I just wish she would come to me," he said with a sad tone.

"Maybe it's because you aren't receptive. I really don't know why she doesn't come to you. It doesn't make sense that I, a stranger, can feel her but you, the love of her life, can't. All I know is that I prayed she'd come to me. At the very least, I wanted to feel her presence."

I continued, "I believe she is using me to let you know she's OK. After so many years of being trapped in that shell of a body, she's *finally* OK."

As we started to move inside, Eric stopped and, with a look of surprise on his face, said, "I'm not sure, but I think this is the exact room we stayed in on our wedding night. I remember we were on the top floor facing the falls, like this. I'd be surprised if it isn't the exact same room. "How..."—his voice broke and he struggled to finish his thought—"...how appropriate that I started my life with her in this room, and now I am ending my life with her here." We held each other and cried.

With this last commemorative event, we both knew that we could move on, taking refuge in the belief that Gaye was in a place with her family who had passed before her. Her memories were now intact, she knew each and every one of her family members again—and she was free to ride horses in the wind. We had also come to understand that in losing a loved one, there would always be hard days yet to endure. But we found comfort in the knowledge that, at last, our bleeding hearts could truly begin to heal.

CHAPTER 21

BLEEDING HEARTS IN BLOOM

I originally began writing my memoirs as a sort of "therapy," never with the intention of writing a book. I am a nurse, not a writer. The idea of turning my writing into a manuscript began nagging at me a couple of months before Eric and I married. When I approached Eric about the idea, he agreed with the thought and supported me 100 percent. I wasn't quite sure how to do it, but I'd give it a shot.

We married October 13, 2010—three years, exactly, from the day we'd met. We married in Ouray, Colorado, at a beautiful Episcopal church. Only the pastor, Eric and I were present. It was how we wanted it: just us.

On the drive to Ouray, from Colorado Springs, I began to wonder as if we were, perhaps, marrying too soon. After all, it hadn't been quite six months since Gaye had passed away. Whenever I had approached Eric about the subject before, he would remind me that he had said good-bye to Gaye a long time ago. I understood what he meant and what he was feeling. But I was so worried about disrespecting Gaye and their marriage.

As we neared our destination, I was deep in silent deliberations when all of a sudden Eric's phone rang. He was busy driving and I answered.

It was Ila. "We're on our way to Ouray right now," I told her.

"That's what I thought, I just wanted to wish you guys the best and tell you that I was thinking about you," she said.

At that point, I couldn't say anything. I felt Gaye; she was with me again. I mumbled some incoherent words to him as I handed him the phone. He looked puzzled that I stopped mid-conversation but took the phone. I can't say I heard him talking to Ila, for I was concentrating deeply on the light so I could be open to what Gaye might have to tell me.

Then I heard her. "It's OK, don't worry anymore. I just want him to be happy. It's all OK." As she left, I felt her love and also a sense of peace that I hadn't experienced in a long time.

As Eric hung up the phone, he looked at me for an explanation about my abrupt ending to my conversation with Ila. He noticed my tears and said, "What's wrong, hon? Why are you crying?" I told him of Gaye's presence and what she wanted us to know. He wrapped his arm around me and hugged me tight.

After we married, we drove back home for our celebratory party with our friends and family the following Saturday. We all needed to celebrate our lives together and the beginning of something new. My children, Eric's children and grandchildren were all in attendance (except for Emily and Megan, as Megan had homecoming that night). I had family come in from out of state; Ila attended, as did both of our parents.

Even my dear ex-father-in-law was there. When I had invited him, he said, "I've never seen you so happy. I love you and really like Eric a lot; of course I will be at your reception." It was truly a celebration and one of the happiest times in my life.

I tried to begin turning my memoirs into a book right after the wedding. But with work, Amanda, home and a new marriage, I found little time to devote to the task of converting recollections into a single story. I played around with it for a while but really couldn't take it seriously with so much on my plate.

Then, in March of 2011, I began to feel an urgency to finish the book or, at the very least, to take it more seriously. I talked to Eric about this pressing feeling one afternoon after we had both arrived home from work. I wasn't sure what the source of the urgency was, but it gnawed at me daily.

Then I felt her again.

Gaye was with me, filling all of my senses with her light; it wasn't as bright as I had once experienced, but the warmth from it was just as powerful. I looked at Eric and, through tear-filled eyes, I told him, "Gaye wants me to finish the manuscript. She's the one making me feel the urgency. She's making me feel as though she doesn't have much time to help me with what she can. She's making me sense that she has to be somewhere, so I need to get the book finished."

As we sat there discussing how I could manage to devote more time to the task, her light never left me. It was then that I told Eric my plans for the proceeds from the published book.

"If, and this is a big if, this book makes any money, I feel that half of the profits should go to a foundation that would be set up in Gaye's name." I paused and sat silent for a moment; I began to feel more tears as well as Gaye's words begin to flow.

"Gaye wants the foundation to be set up to help the families of Alzheimer's victims. She wants them to have whatever they need for support. She's making me feel that she is aware of all the suffering that the families endure. I can't imagine a more perfect way to pay tribute to her, for her part of the story." As soon as had I spoken these words, I felt her leave.

"Well, if that's what you think we should do," Eric said, "then we will."

"No, you don't understand. Gaye wants this. I had always known that I would give half the profits to Alzheimer's, but she is making it clear that it is to be for the support of the family members," I told him.

With this newfound reason for finishing the book, I tried to devote even more time to the manuscript. But it still felt as though my efforts were fruitless, because the manuscript seemed to just inch along.

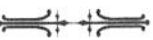

There had been issues in my job that began to make me not want to go to work anymore. I tried to address the matter with supervisors but felt as if there would be no satisfactory resolution. One morning, while sitting at the computer balancing the checkbook, I typed a letter of resignation. I wasn't quite sure where the idea came from. I loved my job. I hated the atmosphere and began dreading going to work, but I had never even thought about writing a letter of resignation. So imagine my surprise when a completed letter stared back at me from the computer monitor. I read the letter over, not remembering typing the words. It was emotion filled and conveyed the feelings of a very unhappy employee.

I decided that I should get Eric's opinion, as well as his consent for me to quit. I emailed it to his work and called him to tell him I sent it. He was just as surprised as I was about the sudden decision to write the letter, but he knew that things were getting worse and that I should move on. He called me back after reading the letter and said, "Send it."

Hitting that "send" button was scary. I have never not worked before. I knew I could find a job again and wasn't worried about being unemployed long. But I also knew that once my employer received this letter, those in charge would make sure that I would never work for their organization again. My "whistle blowing" on the dynamics of the office would be seen as insubordination. But I had to send it, because my job was costing me the joy I felt when taking care of children.

After my resignation, Eric and I decided that my job would be to devote myself to the manuscript. I allocated a specific time of day to writing. The words just flowed. During some of the writing, there are things I wouldn't have known about, such as the visit to the neurologist. I hadn't known Eric and Gaye at this time, and was certainly not present during the visit, but I was able to describe the doctor and his office almost as if I had been there.

When I had written the part about the doctor's office, I printed it on paper. When Eric came home, I had him describe the doctor and his office. I then handed him the pages I had printed. He was floored, to say the least. Everything I wrote was precisely how Eric described it, with one exception: the doctor's name was just a bit off. He was surprised, to say the least, when he read what I had written. This is why I have felt that so much of my writing was Gaye guiding my thoughts and words.

"This was the urgency," I told him that evening. "Gaye had to get her words on paper. She had to help me write of things that I wouldn't know about and that you, perhaps, wouldn't remember or know. I feel that she has somewhere she has to go now, and that was what the urgency was about. I don't know if she'll ever make her presence known to me again. I haven't felt her in a few days," I said, with a sad feeling at speaking the words out loud.

I believe now, and will forever believe, that Gaye came to me and, at least sometimes, is still around me. I believe that she loves me because I chose to stay in the situation out of love for everyone involved.

She understands and knows that I was here for her family as well as for her. I've said it before—I love Gaye; she is a dear family member to me and, everyday, I thank God that he brought me to her and her family.

It is a well-known fact that Gaye had a jealous streak; several different family members told me this. If anyone so much as looked at her husband, her beautiful blue eyes would become strikingly green. Because of her jealous side, some family members have doubted that Gaye would ever have anything but harsh feelings toward me. She would therefore never come to me in the way I have written and the way I have known her to do. But I truly think that jealousy is an earthly emotion, and that we don't carry such negative emotions with us when we die.

Not too long ago, I had a discussion with Madlyn about this very subject. She told me that she had seen Gaye's jealousy and knew of it, firsthand. But she, too, believes that jealousy has no place in heaven, or wherever we go when we die. Madlyn once remarked that if we were to take all the emotions we felt here on Earth with us when we die, we would actually be living in hell. We both chuckled at the comment but believe it to be true.

It is different now. When Gaye is around me, it's much different than her earlier appearances. There is no bright light, but I do feel her love when she's around. I don't pretend to understand it all; I just know how it feels to me. It's as if she talks to me like an old friend. I find myself talking to her as well. I have recently made some purchases of things that, before Gaye's passing, I would never have bought, but they were things that she would have loved. My family, including Eric, thinks it strange. But I know that it's just Gaye sharing herself with me.

It's been a year and a half since she passed away. The family is thriving, though I am certain that they all have their difficult days when they think of Gaye, just as Eric and I do. But somehow we cope with the pain, remember our love for her and keep moving on until, one day, we'll all be together again.

I like to imagine Gaye waiting for me when I pass on, ready to help guide me, for I don't believe we travel alone when we die. I believe that she'll be there, loving me in the way that I loved her throughout her final journey.

In my hope of seeing her then, I also carry the wish that she'll meet me with a big, beautiful bouquet of bleeding hearts.

Made in the USA
Middletown, DE
20 September 2023

38889663R00119